Bara Gali

Iqaluit

Hong Kong
Ithaca

fora

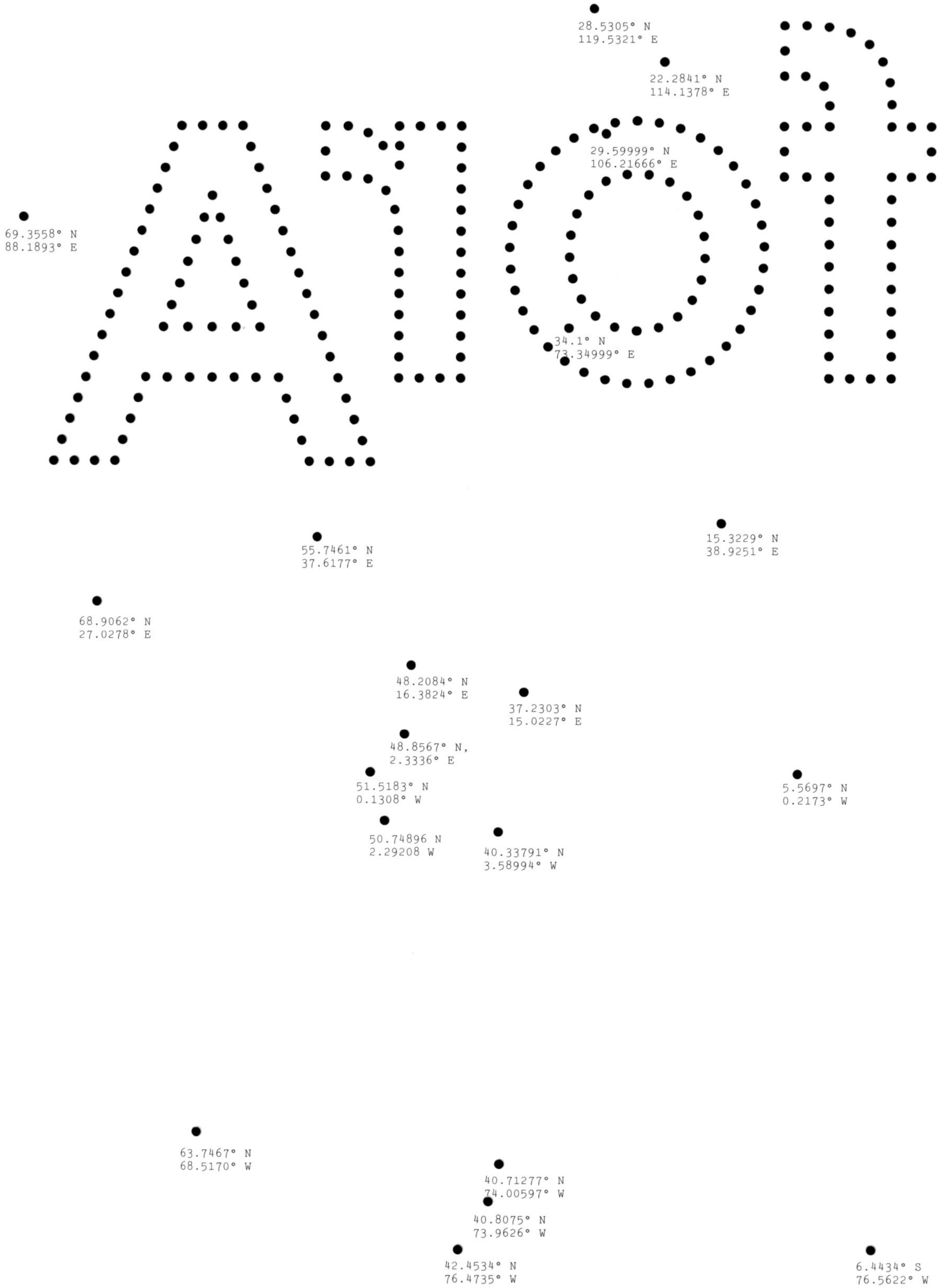
28.5305° N
119.5321° E
22.2841° N
114.1378° E
29.59999° N
106.21666° E
69.3558° N
88.1893° E
34.1° N
73.34999° E
15.3229° N
38.9251° E
55.7461° N
37.6177° E
68.9062° N
27.0278° E
48.2084° N
16.3824° E
37.2303° N
15.0227° E
48.8567° N,
2.3336° E
51.5183° N
0.1308° W
5.5697° N
0.2173° W
50.74896 N
2.29208 W
40.33791° N
3.58994° W
63.7467° N
68.5170° W
40.71277° N
74.00597° W
40.8075° N
73.9626° W
42.4534° N
76.4735° W
6.4434° S
76.5622° W

Vienna
Madrid

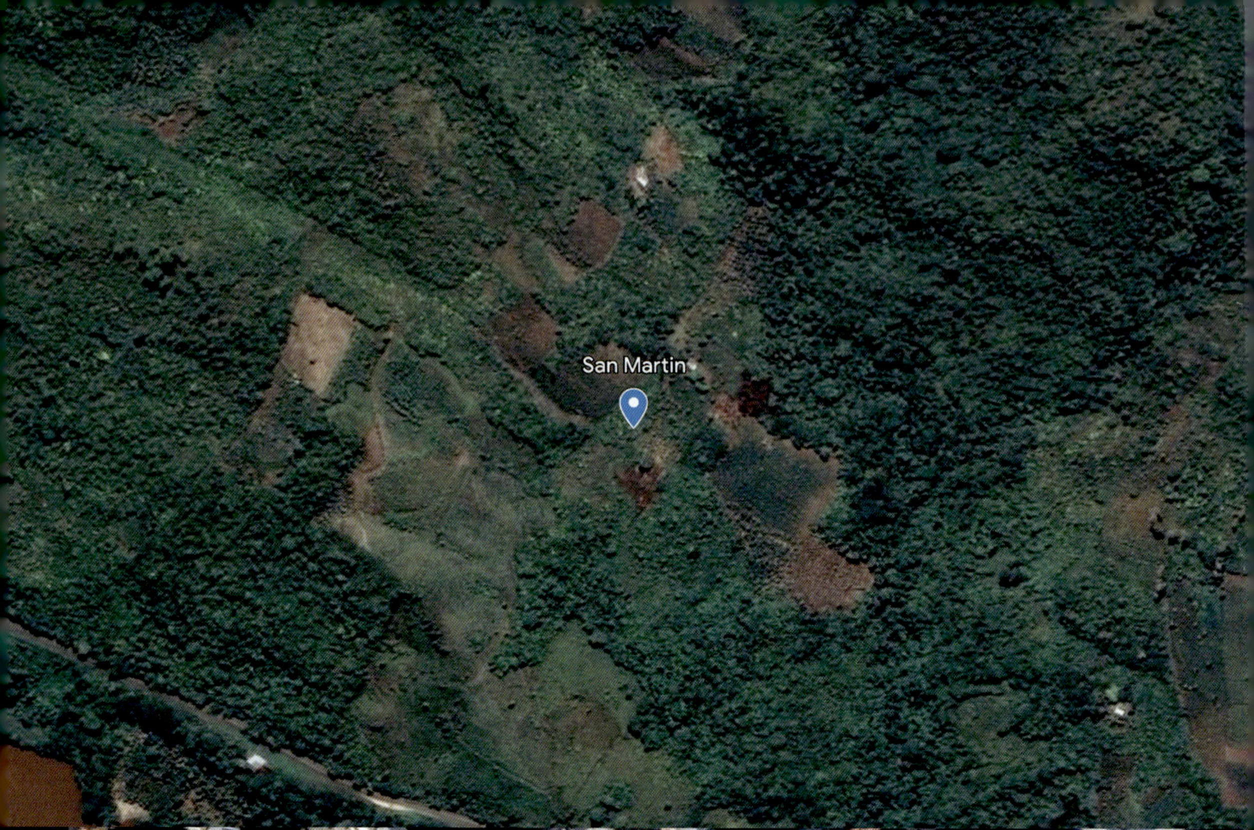
San Martin

Norilsk

Bishan Village

Inari

Accra

Asmara and Aba Shawl

Tolpuddle

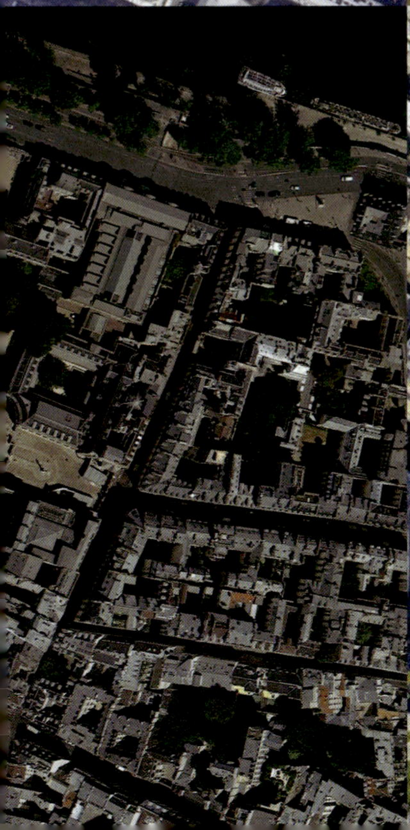

New York

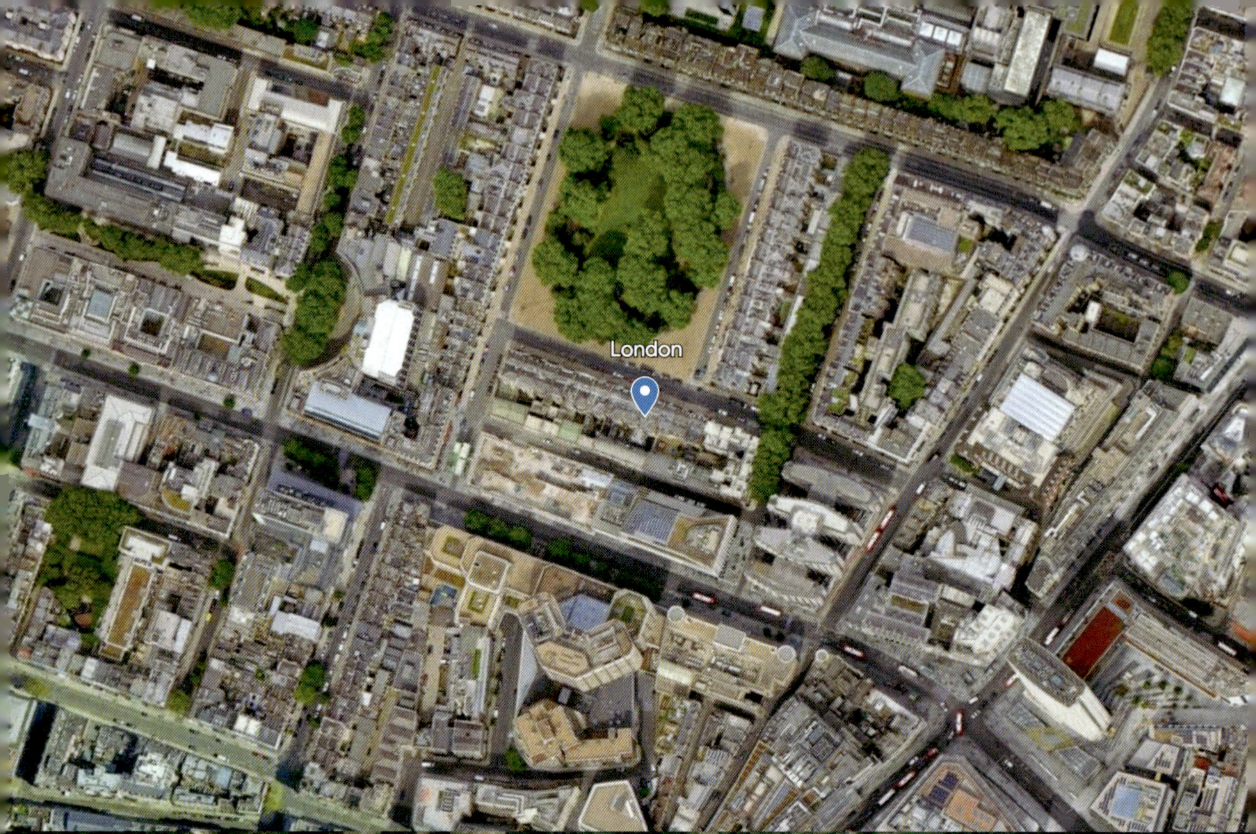
London

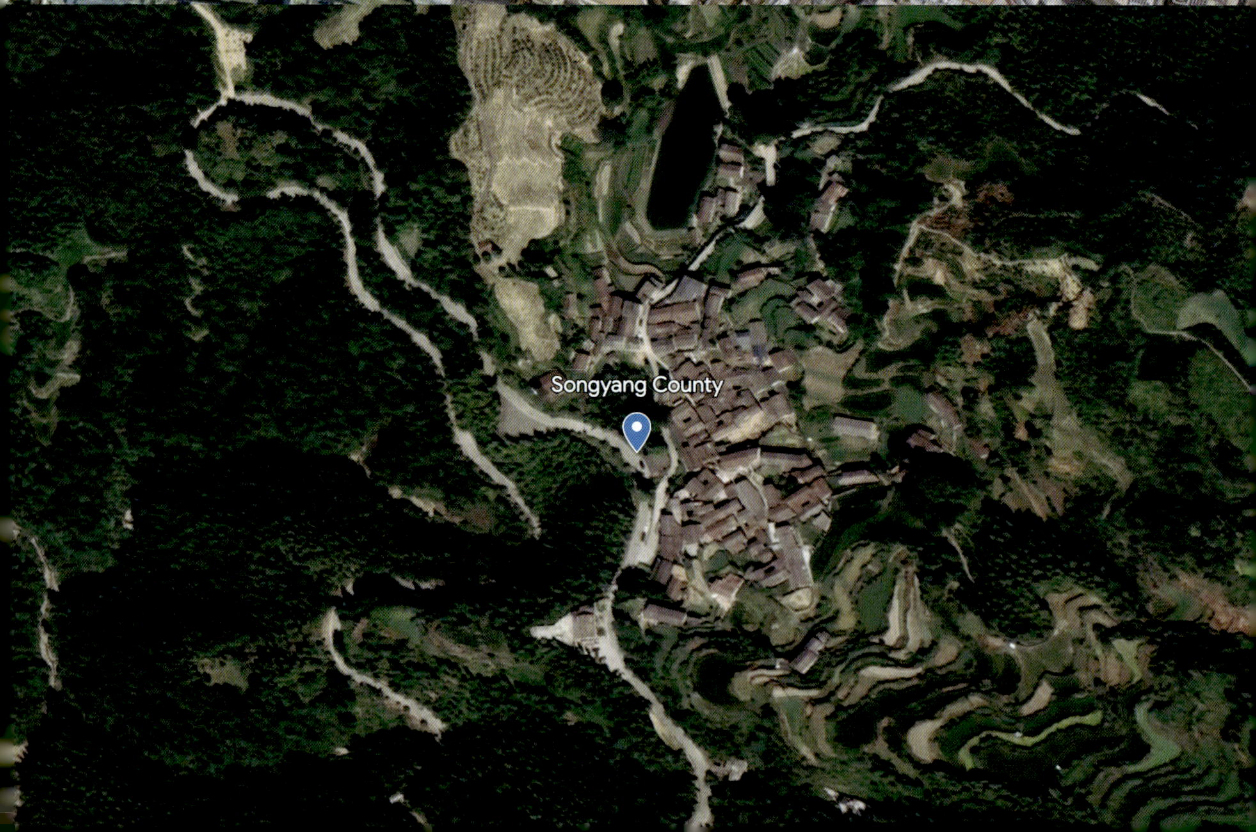
Songyang County

forA on the Urban
Issue #1

Eleven Frictions from an Urbanized World

Birkhäuser
Basel

Andrea Börner, Cristina Díaz Moreno, Efrén García Grinda, Baerbel Mueller,
Institute of Architecture at the University of Applied Arts Vienna (Eds.)

Table of Contents

14 Introduction
(3 min read)

17 The Mix
Keller Easterling
(5 min read)

25 20 Pesewas and Sound
Steloo
(6 min read)

31 Six Frictions
Phineas Harper
(7 min read)

41 Crossing the Riverbanks
Alexia León
(9 min read)

47 How to Love a Tree (a Lament)
Hira Nabi
(10 min read)

57 Reviving the Rural
Xu Tiantian in conversation with Ou Ning
(10 min read)

67 Moscow, a City of Mutual Silence
Konstantin Kim
(10 min read)

77 Diary of an Accumulation
Nasrine Seraji
(12 min read)

85 When Walls Speak to Us
Santiago Cirugeda and María Paz Núñez Martí
(12 min read)

105 Architecture's Non-Nested and Elastic Scales
Lola Sheppard and Mason White
(15 min read)

117 Visions for Architectural Demodernization
Emilio Distretti and Alessandro Petti
Photographs by Luca Capuano
(15 min read)

Introduction

At long last, we seem to have come to terms with understanding the urban not only as an all-encompassing conception of the earth, but also as an inevitable and crucial seismograph that reminds us of life in the world with all its concrete facets.

forA on the Urban examines the open, unfinished, multiscaled, interconnected, complex, and wild nature of urban manifestations, challenges, and situations through an expanded notion of architecture. Following issue #0, which sought to open up the wider field of the urban in order to provide initial orientation, thinking, and material, issue #1 is dedicated to the subject of friction—concrete and tangible phenomena that can be localized to distinct coordinates around the globe. As diverse or similar as these sites may appear in aerial imagery, so too are the particular narratives of frictions to which they relate, identify, give rise, or, likewise, remain hidden, unnoticed, or occluded.

This compilation brings together projects, views, positions, and perspectives from a diverse range of voices—architects, urbanists, designers, visual and performing artists, curators, political activists, critics, and theorists—from a variety of backgrounds and locales. Every contribution collected is discrete in terms of its angle of approach, the friction(s) it addresses, and the material through which it speaks. At the same time, common threads interweave the ideas explored in multiple ways throughout the works, suggesting that the more specific the challenge, subject, place, or perspective, the more commonalities it can hold.

Advocating "The Mix," Keller Easterling sweeps away the mechanisms of knowledge production and monolithic thinking since the Enlightenment and gives room to personalities, dissenters, and activists who have yet to have their say in mainstream academic discourse. Addressing the sensorial multitude of urban spaces with his audiovisual piece "20 Pesewas and Sound," Steloo composes a tapestry of sound from Accra, capturing not only aural resonances but the visual traces of iconic audible objects, all of which—sometimes overlooked and overheard—contribute to the identity of the city. In "Six Frictions," Phineas Harper glides through partially counter-intuitive but thoroughly plausible notions of friction in the UK: movement, technology, industry, social justice, history, culture, material, structure, infrastructure, mobility, AI, tools, rental markets, demographics, planning, politics, and—still among many other things—cows. As Harper puts it, "No friction, no movement": without an abundance of friction there is no potential for change. Exploring the co-existence of human settlements and the woods, Alexia León delves deep into the Peruvian Andean Amazon with her project "Atlas Río Mayo," walking the *waman samanas* landscape with members of the Kichwa Lamas, encountering the city as forest. Artist Hira Nabi develops a kinship with two trees in the Bara Gali forest outside of Murree, Pakistan, in "How to Love a Tree (a Lament)," tracing both arboreal and human trauma in their trunks. In a conversation addressing the impact of China's urbanization on its rural areas, curator and artist Ou Ning and architect Xu Tiantian expand on their experiences working with local communities to revive villages in Songyang County and Bishan. Konstantin Kim investigates cultural complexities of the urban in "Moscow, a City of Mutual Silence" as he looks at the capital's recent past to make sense of the attitudes of its citizens of present. Drawing an arc from subjective engagement to the political dimension of the post-Soviet condition, he explores the spaces that have manifested as a result. In "Diary of an Accumulation" Nasrine Seraji reflects on frictions in architectural education and practice over a period of six decades and across three continents, revealing that spatial events can shape a person as much as a place. "When Walls Speak to Us," by Santiago Cirugeda and María Paz Núñez-Márti, presents a different kind of site-specific accumulation of frictions: the graffitied walls of Cañada Real Galiana, Europe's largest slum, which serve as canvases for expression, indicating separation while simultaneously seeking to connect the worlds of those who impose measures and those who measure through experience. Revealing interconnected frictions of highly local and vast territorial spatial stories in "Architecture's Non-Nested and Elastic Scales," Lola Sheppard and Mason White question the value of scaled drawings, and examine the fallacies and potentials of mapping techniques in rural and remote areas in the Arctic Circle and along e-waste streams. Finally, Emilio Distretti and Alessandro Petti, with accompanying photographs by Luca Capuano, share their "Visions for Architectural Demodernization," narrated through the related histories of seemingly disparate sites: Aba Shawl, set within the modernist city of Asmara and the first Indigenous urban settlement of Eritrea, and several former fascist rural colonies, or *borghi*, of Sicily.

While each contribution stands on its own—reflecting particular circumstances, situations, dilemmas, engagements, observations, or thoughts—together they add up to a kaleidoscopic view of spatial frictions that have resulted in imbalances, exclusions, or negotiations, as much as identity construction, economic booms, or the emergence of multiplicity, plurality, and co-existence.

The Mix

(5 min read)

New York
40.7128° N, 74.0060° W

Keller Easterling

Culture often stubbornly searches for singular evils and singular solutions. The residual White Enlightenment mind exalts the one and only and believes it can only generate thought through a dialectic progression of opposing forces towards an ultimate. In this hierarchical world of dualisms and warring binaries, ideation must assume the structure of religious fairy tales. Stories must have conflict as their engine. Legal forms must exist as arguments. Quantifications proceed through axiomatic expressions towards a proof. This is the apparatus of reasonable thinking. It is treated as a form of sophistication rather than a primitive blunt instrument.

Project an image of Karl Marx next to Peter Kropotkin, or Gabriel Tarde, and, even though the line-up is restricted to white men, most populations of college students will only be able to identify Marx. And even if the others can be named, they will likely be regarded as supporting characters and minor texts in relation to the lead role. It is a culture that would seize on and create what Vilém Flusser called "textolatry" around one thinker who must have the solution.[1] For the Enlightenment mind, just opening the door to others might be seen as an attempt to depose Marx and put a rival in his place! But this is just a symptom of the same stubborn habit of mind that, making a category mistake, confuses part with whole. Thinking in

1 Vilém Flusser, *Toward a Philosophy of Photography*, trans. Anthony Mathews (London: Reaktion Books, 2000), 3–4.

this way, multiple markets will be treated as one market that must be crushed and comprehensively replaced. Activist positions must demand that followers are either for them or against them, and phrases like "speaking with one voice," seem to appear by default. There is only one fight on which all other fights rely.

The entirely reasonable rationale for this all-or-nothing approach is that compromise or centrist positions only bolster power and maintain the status quo, and yet the all-or-nothing position may also strengthen even more dangerous forms of power. The single evil, single solution, single ideology approach makes it easier for political superbugs who deploy populist or authoritarian tactics. Recognizing the acculturated success of singular gods and binary fights, superbugs scramble and conflate ideological positions as they harvest loyalties, incite violence, and establish themselves as that god.

Meanwhile, there is no singular evil but rather a spectrum of dangers from capitalism, fascism, racism, whiteness, xenophobia, sectarian violence, religious intolerance, caste, femicide, sociopathic leadership, and countless other means hoarding authoritarian power while oppressing others and abusing the planet. Human agents have also passed off their power to many non-human agents.
The spectrum keeps forming familiar mixtures of whiteness, imperialism, settler colonialism, racialized capital, and labor abuse. And those

sewing the clothes, mining the minerals, sitting on the exhausted land, or facing the fire and water are often people of color or other victims of the extremes of inequality. Still, as the various dangers come braided and temporarily allied in different combinations, at any one time, the ideologies used to describe them may or may not catch all of their disguises and modes for camouflage.

Just as there are no singular evils, there is no correct form of dissent. Activism is advocating, rioting, marching, looting, blockading, boycotting, sanctioning, sabotaging, and divesting, among many other things. Nothing changes without pressure. Sometimes, the most forceful activism is the gentlest response to the environment violence and damage caused by powers that demolish, poison, abuse, subjugate, erase you not just with a gunshot or a drawn sword but with fossil fuels, sheltered wealth, monopolies of data, murderous policing. But to declare a correct way to protest is a weak position. Those who do may also come from a position of privilege that does not risk death when speaking out—that does not require forms of fugitivity to survive. And activism also requires the sneakiness to double-cross the political superbugs who run rings around singular solutions and singular evils. Dissensus is stronger when there is a mixture of techniques to keep the superbugs guessing, starved, and disoriented.

Setting aside monolithic thinking and broadening of the activist repertoire redoubles the potential territory for dissensus. Luckily, the seminal figures of textolatry are quickly overtaken by the abundance of thinkers on the other side of White Enlightenment thought. Those who have been the victims of so much of its harm are often offering the most potent counter-logics and antidotes. The swell of voices from abolitionist, anarchist, feminist, Black, Brown, and Indigenous thinkers suggests that, as Ruth Wilson Gilmore has asserted, "abolition is a horizon." To redress injustices, something more like a field condition or broad gradient of varied activities and multiple fronts? Might it even mean that abolition is not infinitely delayed but coming more quickly? Power is not replaced but overwhelmed by multiple approaches that do not adhere to the mono-ideational belief or the binary fight.

That same abundance of thinkers, scholars, and activists meets a contemporary opportunity for solidarity—one that recalls the international solidarity between the Pan-African, Non-Aligned, Tricontinental, and civil rights movements in the twentieth century. The work of Adom Getachew, Anne G. Mahler, or David Featherstone, or Cynthia Anne Young tell the stories of these exiles, government leaders, intellectuals, writers, activists, and artists who built an international network during a wave of colonial independence and just prior to a neoliberal turn. While that moment of solidarity was crushed by late-twentieth-century neoliberal forces that further tilted the playing field in favor of established power, a contemporary wave of solidarity potentially moves beyond the international to the planetary.

These histories align with other rafts of thinkers for whom space animates another way of being human beyond dominant cultural habits. They meet historians of Black Radicalism, Pan-Africanism and Black Pastoralism like Robin D. G. Kelley, Russell Rickford, and Edward Onaci. And these link to the histories of Black cooperative movements from Jessica Gordon Nembhard, Greta de Jong, or Monica M. White. Spatial variables counter the thin abstractions of capital with tangible, heavy, lumpy values to do with position, proximity, solids, and sequence. These are the very networks of care, maintenance, mutualism, and kinship that activists—among them Ruth Wilson Gilmore, Mariame Kaba, Silvia Federici, Fred Moten, Denise Ferreira da Silva, Saidiya V. Hartman, Tiffany Lethabo King, Katherine McKittrick, and Sylvia Wynter—have called for as alternatives to monocultures of all sorts. These are the spaces that J. K. Gibson-Graham calls "community economies" or the "convivial" forms of commoning between human and nonhumans that move away from the modern and towards Arturo Escobar's pluriverse.

And Olúfẹ́mi O. Táíwò imagines extending to a planetary scale the special sovereignties that Black, Brown, and Indigenous people have developed to cope with whiteness.

If the international or global thinking of mid-century tended toward universals and ideological consistency, maybe the planetary tends towards the partial and multiple world that is impossible to parse with an elementary particle. It is a world that Anna Tsing and others might describe as "patchy" or related to a refreshed notion of indigeneity that retools disciplinary thought.[2] She notes that "In contrast to Enlightenment universals, international indigenous politics opens a global politics in which inconsistency and contradiction become our greatest assets. ... Still, indigenous victories depend on mismatching universal rights and local cultural legacies, expert science and place-based knowledge, social justice, and communal precedence."[3]

This inconsistency aligns with the need to create a broad dissensus or a moving target to confuse authoritarian power, but it also addresses the multitude of diverse situated ecologies in the world. There are pockets of activism that do not register within the logics of whiteness, hierarchy, monism, and binary and are often surrounding hostility at their borders. And everywhere is a multitude of

2 Anna Tsing, Andrew S. Mathews, and Nils Bubandt, "Patchy Anthropocene: Landscape Structure, Multispecies History, and the Retooling of Anthropology: An Introduction to Supplement 20" in Patchy Anthropocene: Frenzies and Afterlives of Violent Simplifications, *Current Anthropology* 60, no. S20 (August 2019).

3 Anna Tsing, "Indigenous Voice," in *Indigenous Experience Today*, ed. Marisol de la Cadena and Orin Starn, (London: Taylor & Francis Group, 2007), 57.

problems and conditions that do not conform to dominant habits. Those problems have often fallen off the ledgers of financializing, taxonomizing, digitizing abstraction that dominant culture constructs. They are the “failures” or the lumpy fallout—the weeds that are all different but growing everywhere. And they are an abundant resource of vitality that is always available. Capital is not the only system to be comprehensively replaced by another system. Instead, multiple problems and modes of exchange can overwhelm monocultures of all sorts.

Friction is a distributed condition with multiple fronts and multiple methods. Activists sometimes shoot the weeds in the field, sometimes change something in the soil, and sometimes just let the weeds grow. These are all forms of direct action although some are more environmental, dispositional, or spatial. Maybe designers are not only designing objects and systems, but agile forms of interplay that respond to potentials. Design innovations are not just new technologies or contours, but a scheme for how these things interact and go together in the mix.

Keller Easterling is a writer, designer, and the Enid Storm Dwyer Professor of Architecture at Yale. Her books include *Medium Design* (Verso 2021), *Extrastatecraft: The Power of Infrastructure Space* (Verso, 2014), *Subtraction* (Sternberg, 2014), *Enduring Innocence: Global Architecture and its Political Masquerades* (MIT, 2005), and *Organization Space: Landscapes, Highways and Houses in America* (MIT, 1999). She also co-authored (with Richard Prelinger) *Call it Home*, a laserdisc/DVD history of US suburbia from 1934–1960. She lectures, publishes, and exhibits internationally. Her work appeared in the 2014 and 2018 Venice Biennales, and she was a 2019 United States Artist in Architecture and Design.

20 Pesewas and Sound

(6 min read)

Accra
5.5697° N, 0.2173° W

Steloo

The Tradition goes on. Oral communication plays an integral part of the sound identity through the mother tongue of the people of Accra. Over time, urbanization has impacted the identity of the language and sounds of the Ga—the traditional Indigenous settlers and people of Accra.

The beautiful chaos observed as part of the everyday life of the people of Accra oozes a unique sonic tapestry woven by the urban, socio-economic experiences, struggles, and triumphs—an experience filtered through my lens and expressed in this collection of images and sound.

Field recordings capture the sound-print of the environment and are processed to open up a new dialogue. Iconic objects and forms that replicate sound patterns and tones—most of which go overlooked—are captured through sound that documents, holds, and interacts with the everyday of Accra. Most of these visuals and sounds are seen as chaotic noise.

This chaotic noise of friction holds the importance of communal identity within the urban spaces of Accra. Through my real-life immersion and interactions in the community, the community becomes an audience to

Street
noise

Honking
cars

Street
noise

Trotro conductor
calling passengers:
“Accra, Accra”

“Accra
Accra”

Honking
cars

Honking
cars

“Accra
Accra”

10 a.m.
Bus station
megaphone
broadcasting
destinations

Honking
cars

Taxi passenger
bangs car door

Ocean
waves

Ocean
waves

something that they have always been an audience of, without notice. My intention was to unlock and reveal this identity by shifting the visual language using sound and form as a device of communication.

The art of looking at chaos within the urban in a positive way becomes a path that leads to the discovery of the overlooked by implementing abstraction and experimentation as a raw filter in this soundscape of storytelling, enriching the skills within local oral urbanism and highlighting the beauty of chaos through sound and objects.

As a practitioner of sound, I encourage Accra locals to become their own sound architects in constructing a meaningful oral soundscape that shapes their urban life.

My work explores an inherent symbiosis between the interactivity experienced when oral skills are used to build a community and when a community builds the oral soundscape of the city and its inhabitants.

Take the time to discover the hidden layers, textures, and tones of soundscapes that this unique experience of urban conflict, language, and belonging have inspired.

Ocean waves

People talking

Market noise

Boy calling a brother

Fisherman preparing net and singing

Sounds of crickets and frogs at night

Mosques calling prayers, 10 a.m.

Bus station megaphone broadcasting

Church members praying & singing praises

Girl sweeping

Mobile fish monger selling in the neighbourhood

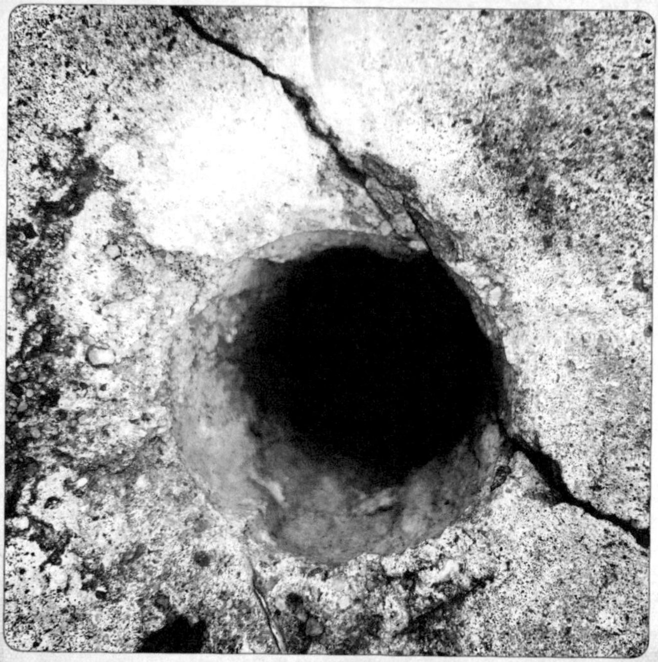

Earth's Resonance

Habitation Motifs

"Mineral" Bottles as Aerophones and Idiophones

Poetry in Heartbreak

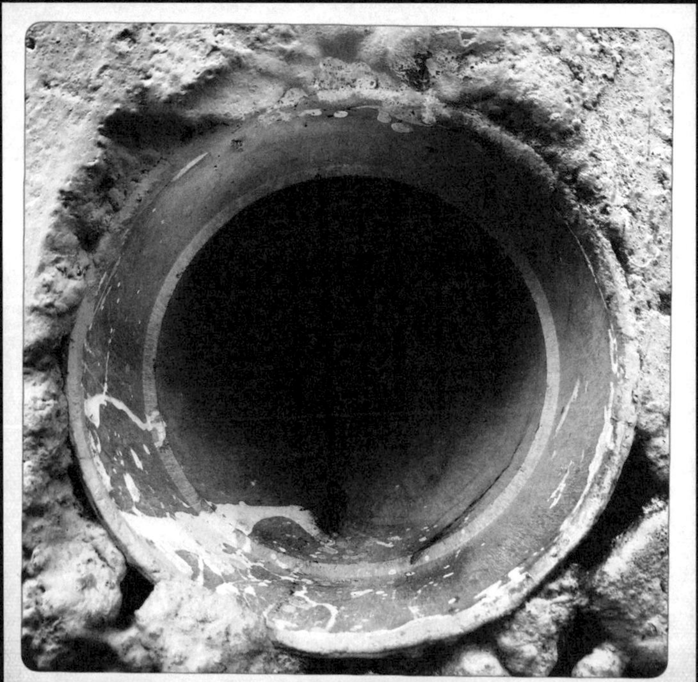

Reverberation

Listen to the audio:
www.fora-ontheurban.net/contribut
/20-Pesewas-and-Sound-Steloo

Steloolive (Evans Mireku Kissi) i
performance artist, composer, and
music DJ based in Accra, Ghana. W
eccentric style of exploring soun
trailblazer of his generation. Hi
consists of a mixture of experime
delivery, fashion, art, and conce
photography.

Six Frictions

(7 min read)

Tolpuddle
50.748968° N, 2.292084° W

Phineas Harper

Movement

"What causes a moving car to slow down? And don't tell me it's friction." There's a certain breed of teacher who seems to resent the ignorance of their pupils like a doctor sick of ill people. A home-ed kid, I was mostly spared the barked questions of secondary school, but on finally enrolling at sixteen, I had nowhere to hide. "Air resistance?" I guessed, which seemed to appease my physics teacher. "Close enough," he conceded, almost as relieved as I was. "Friction, of course," he told us, "is what causes a car to move."

Friction is indeed what causes cars to move. The drilling of oil and its refinement to petrol, the mining and smelting of ore to make the steel in combustion engines, the robotic arms flanking production lines—the entire automobile industry depends on mastering the all-important coefficient of friction between rubber tires on asphalt. No friction, no movement.

Progress

On Friday June 12, 1799, William Pitt (Britain's youngest-ever prime minister) passed the Combination Act, banning workers from collectivizing. Three decades later in Tolpuddle, Methodist preacher and farmhand George Loveless was arrested and deported along with five others for the crime of swearing an oath to work for no less than ten shillings a week. News of the sentence triggered public outcry and, in an age long before even radio communication, a protest petition of 800,000 signatures was delivered to parliament. The 'Tolpulddle Martyrs' became folk heroes—symbols of the tension between ordinary people and their ruling oppressors.

But the story has a happy ending. As an old man, Loveless lived to see the 1871 Trade Union Act finally sweep away Pitt's legacy and enfranchise the role of unionism in British society, solidifying the kernel of contemporary labor law. Loveless and the Tolpuddle Martyrs are a blunt reminder that every decent facet of Britain's liberal-ish democratic-ish economy has been won through struggle, sometimes encompassing centuries of class friction. Minimum wages, statutory leave, sick pay, and even weekends had to be prised into existence against powerful resistance. Nothing gets better without a fight.

Structure

A typical block of limestone has a compressive strength of around 100 N/mm^2. Crushed, heated beyond one thousand degrees, sintered to clinker, ground to cement, mixed with aggregates and water, and cast in formwork as concrete, the new block will now have a compressive strength closer to 40 N/mm^2. All those processes, all that energy (cement production alone accounts for seven percent of global greenhouse gas emissions), all that effort to make a material less than half as strong as the original limestone—why?

Many contemporary designers find stone synonymous with antiquity—a cumbersome and inherently traditionalist material best left for high-end kitchen workshops and pseudo-Georgian facades. But if stone performs more highly gram for gram than concrete, isn't it time to take it more seriously as a potential super material of the future? Stone architecture built without mortar can be found across the world, from the humble drystone walls of Scottish shepherds to the enormous temples of Greek and Incan civilizations. Great Zimbabwe, a ninth-century city spanning seven square kilometers, housed around 18,000 people at its peak within mighty stone walls. Over a millennium later, those walls still stand because the lack of mortar gives the architecture flexibility, allowing movement during earth tremors even as friction keeps the stack of stones from sliding apart. Working with raw stone rather than concrete and cement, the great masons of the past used friction to make remarkable structures that have endured many centuries longer than the expected lifetimes of contemporary buildings.

Revolution

The following text was generated by an AI fed the prompt, "write about friction in the style of political and architectural critic, Phineas Harper."

> In architecture, friction has a long and complex history. From the earliest structures made of mud and wood, to the most advanced engineering feats of the modern age, friction has been used to control movement and shape the built environment. At the most basic level, friction is used to keep parts of a structure together, by providing an opposing force to the forces of gravity and other external forces. In urban planning, friction is also an important concept. Friction is used to slow down or prevent unwanted movements, such as the flow of traffic in a city. By introducing obstacles that make it difficult to move from one point to another, planners can control the overall movement of people and vehicles. Friction is thus a powerful tool in the hands of architects and urban planners. By harnessing friction, we can shape our environments and create vibrant urban spaces.

The text is not especially profound, but the free online AI churned it out in less than ten seconds. Other than a telltale "thus" in the penultimate sentence (a word only AIs and the most pretentious academics still use), it's a fairly good impression of my writing style, complete with a heavy-handed attempt to link ancient and contemporary construction techniques, and an unearned emotive conclusion. In 2023 AI writing bots jumped from generating amusing but rarely convincing copy to outputs that are almost indistinguishable from those authored by humans. Soon, droves of copywriters will be losing their jobs to machine learning software as free tools make it possible to automate ever more writing assignments. Will the coming industrial revolution in automation emancipate thousands, allowing radical improvements in employment conditions, or push more workers into precarity while shareholders soak up the profits of cost-cutting? How can even a well-organized union of writers take collective action against The Cloud? The friction between human and machine is mounting towards a bitter conflict.

Escalation

The first London Underground line opened in 1906 with a strapline declaring it the "coolest place to be" in hot weather thanks to the 14°C clay surrounding its tunnels, but bit by bit the Tube has been warming up. Heat, particularly from the friction created by trains braking at stations, has been incrementally warming the tunnels for over a century. The clay surrounding the Central Line is now more than 26°C, and air temperatures in the tunnels reach over 35°C every summer (the legal limit for transporting cows, sheep, and pigs in the EU is 30°C). Six-figure cash prizes have been offered to anyone who can devise a solution to cool the tunnels, but until they do, the temperature will keep rising.

Crisis

Recently, Mayor of London Sadiq Khan called an emergency summit to tackle the rent crisis sweeping the capital. In 2023 alone, London rents were on track to rise 15.8% as landlords take advantage of the UK's incredibly weak regulations that offer renters no meaningful protection from exploitation. The crisis underscores how generational housing inequality has become central to the politics of the UK which is now more profoundly polarized by age than any other demographic. Older Brits, whether traditionally middle- or working-class, are largely secure in their housing, having bought homes at low prices in the 70s, 80s, and 90s and enjoyed extraordinary rises in land values ever since. Younger renters, meanwhile, are trapped, frequently forced to hand over upwards of half their income to their aging landlords.

The old and wealthy generation is collectively ransacking the livelihoods of the young, greedily creaming off the proceeds of their labor while denying them the stability to put down roots or start families. As the grubbing of this all-out intergenerational class war grows more fractious, it is increasingly reflected in national polls, with age now directly correlating to voting preference. If retirees were excluded from the electorate and only those of working age permitted a vote, Rishi Sunak (Britain's richest-ever prime minister) and his ruling Conservative Party would be annihilated overnight.

Last year an inquest ruled that four-year-old Awaab Ishak died from exposure to mold in his rented house. The complaints of his heartbroken young parents were repeatedly ignored by their disinterested housing association landlord. For societies elsewhere, the lesson is clear: housing is an essential commodity that should never be allowed to slip into deregulated profiteering as it has in the UK. The British rent crisis is nothing short of a catastrophe, pushing a generation into economic servitude, killing children, and breaking any sense of a social contract.

Some architects will say the solution is more housing construction, but there are already more empty second homes than homeless people in Britain, and new census data has revealed that prices have been rising even in neighborhoods where populations have fallen, proving that the normal rules of supply and demand disintegrated long ago.

Without friction, wheels cannot grip the road to drive vehicles forward. Without friction, the story of Loveless and the Tolpuddle Martyrs cannot not grip the public spirit, driving the cause of unionism forward. Like small stones in a mighty wall standing firm against the centuries, the weak are made stronger by the shared friction that holds them together—able to weather even tremors that shake their foundations. Friction brings conflict and the heat of escalation, but the only hope of ending our housing crisis is that the tension between generations will continue to mount until it snaps, forcing the political change needed to restore dignity to Britain's young. Nothing gets better without a fight.

Phineas Harper is a kinetic sculptor, architecture critic, and chief executive of Open City. They curated the 2019 Oslo Architecture Triennale on the architecture of degrowth and are a regular host of the Londown podcast. They co-founded the New Architecture Writers program, which supports young people from underrepresented communities to pursue careers as design critics, and Turncoats, a debating series mixing architecture and stand-up comedy. Their writing has been published in the *Guardian*, the *Independent*, *Domus*, *Harvard Design Magazine*, and the *Literary Review*. They live on a council estate in southeast London and have two cats, Kaspar and Alvar.

Crossing the Riverbanks[1]

(9 min read)

San Martín
6.4434° S, 76.5622° W

Alexia León

Chimpa. lado opuesto, la otra banda[2]
Chimpa. bandear, chimbar el río
Chimba. aku chimbaypa kay yakuta: vamos a bandear este río[3]

Chimpa. s. Banda
Chimpay. Cruzar un río, chimbar, vadear[4]

1 An answer to "For A Questionnaire. All Cities Contain 'Others'" (Lesley Lokko, 2021) which arose from the Atlas Río Mayo research in the Peruvian Andean Amazon (Leon, 2019).

2 Chimpa. The opposite riverbank
Chimpa. To ford the river
Chimba. aku chimbaypa kay yakuta: Let's ford this river
Chimpa. n. Riverbank
Chimpay. To ford a river

3 Gerald Taylor, *Diccionario normalizado y comparativo: Chachapoyas-Lamas* (Paris: L'Harmattan, 1979).

4 Marinell Park, Nancy Weber, and Victor Cenepo Sangama, *Diccionario Quechua, San Martín* (Lima: Ministry of Education, 1976).

(FIG. 1)
A *campo* at Atlas Río Mayo, 2018

To say "I'm going to the riverbank" at a specific position on the Mayo River is to name everything that is in front of us; it requires creating a synthesis of diversity in constant mutation. The riverbank is a territorial synthesis of everything that happens over there, in front of where I am. In the absence of this physical articulation between riverbanks, the *waman samanas*[5] landscape would probably not exist. This landscape, sparked off by the "situated" memory, generates the political direction attached to territory. These visions create the syntax for its reproduction: an articulated route of assessments and decisions, where a shared territoriality is exercised by a collective with a specific materiality, ethic, and aesthetics. In a closely knit community of "others" there is an exchange of local knowledge; the relationship between an internal community network and external forces that exert daily pressures is discussed and challenged through collaboration centered on altering the environment. The restoration of the forest network, the acknowledgment of territorial vulnerability, and the possibility of resilience are discussed with newcomers. Here, at the *samanas* or *samanitas*,[6] when you are not walking, the collective territorial vision arises. Directions of resistance are traced together through an environmental, consensual view, in order to regulate the territories' alterations. The *waman samanas* landscape is linked to interscalar mobility and micro, dynamic territories with porous borders, which are constantly transformed by different socio-natural ties (León, 2019).

The most thrilling urban/territorial experience I have ever undergone was my year in the heart of the Andean Amazon, in Peru's San Martín Region, walking and resting in the *waman samanas* with mestizo and native Kichwa Lamas community leaders. We were working together on the Atlas Río Mayo Project, striving to understand specific local notions of territory and landscape. Crossing the Mayo riverbanks, we were always surrounded by mountains, on the eastern side of the Andean range. In the heart of northern Peru, "urban" not only implies valley-devouring buildings, such as we see in Lima, defined by precise administrative limits and property lines; the word can also refer to a multi-situated physical configuration, connected by a system of paths and water trails organized along limits of maintenance and care between community members, through a constant collective modification of interconnected environments. The experience of walking through the riverbanks with Kichwa Lamas walkers showed me that multi-situated houses, orchards, forests, and water habitats are connected by time-shift technologies linked to an ecological history, a knowledge of multiple physical collaborations attuned to the unexpected circumstances and desires of being close to others, of shaping life with newcomers through temporary alliances. The sun, the moon,

5 "*Waman-samanas* are a network of rest stations with specific geographic locations linked to the intersection of the main ridges (*filos*) and bridle paths connected to trails between the Mayo riverbanks." Alexia León, ed., *Atlas Río Mayo. Territorio dinámico y paisaje inter-escalar waman-samanas en la Amazonía del Perú. Caso de estudio: Comunidades en red Bajo Mayo: Flores del Río Mayo, San Antonio del Río Mayo, Churuyacu del Río Mayo y Solo del Río Mayo. Lamas, San Martín* (Masters thesis, Pontificia Universidad Católica del Peru, 2019).

6 "Flat stones lie on the ground on widening esplanades off the main trails, providing resting spaces for the community." Ibid.

the stars, the birds, and the trees are part of this everyday project centered on community, which always deals creatively with conflict and affection. The act itself of walking through the chacra-huerto culture became an intertwining of agriculture and architecture, in a way that dissolves the colonial-modern notions of “urban” and “rural.” The Amazon is no more the outskirts of a green void, flush with resources and empty of people, encircling the privileged urban centers of modern and progress consumption. The Amazon is, rather, a multiple, multicultural conservation project, undertaken by people in synchronicity, people that still believe in mutual support through cooperative tools, despite their differences and generational viewpoints. Within these micro-territories, with porous borders, questions about economy, education, policies, and planning collide, as well as issues regarding race, equity, gender, and identity, among others. What is relevant today is understanding that forests contain multiple cities and network communities—both local and migrant—brimming with new others. These multiple dynamic identity forces are building the contemporary Amazon through a territorial educational project that believes in civic territorial governance. This has transformed my perspective on cities and forests; it has pointed me toward collective action processes for the future of our practice as architects/urban planners. Acquiring a decolonized territorial knowledge is urgent, both in my country and elsewhere; it requires practitioners and educators to be in contact with new tools for thinking/making, as well as a new understanding of a time for action which centers on the common good, rather than one predetermined by alienation. The blind, blistering pace of urban processes, detached from the reality of the ground, is part of today’s cultural and environmental degradation. A shift in perspective is of the essence; our planet requires us to think of territorial education as the new matrix for a new physical engagement.

These eight drawn sections help me to remember the complexity of a concrete social reality, even if outdated and incomplete, in addition to being transformed through socio-natural exchanges impossible to represent on paper. (FIGS. 2–9) Drawing these sections that show the great leaps in scale between riverbanks led me to reflect not only on the dynamics of change that shape specific territories and landscapes but also on the will of community integration, on the project of restoration as a priority.

← (FIGS. 2–9)

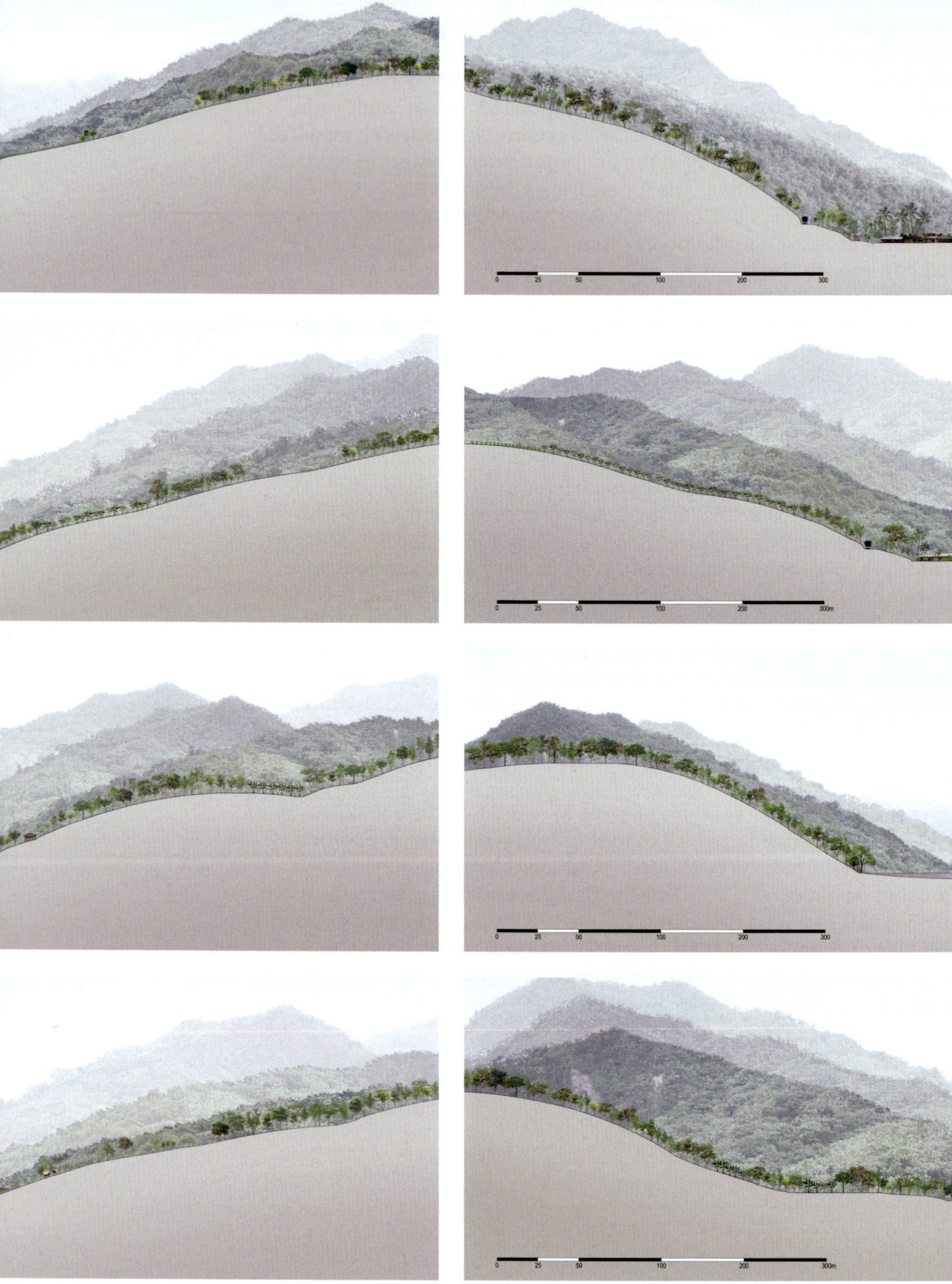

as the Kichwa Lamas native community of Solo del Río Mayo in Lamas (San Martín Region, Peru)

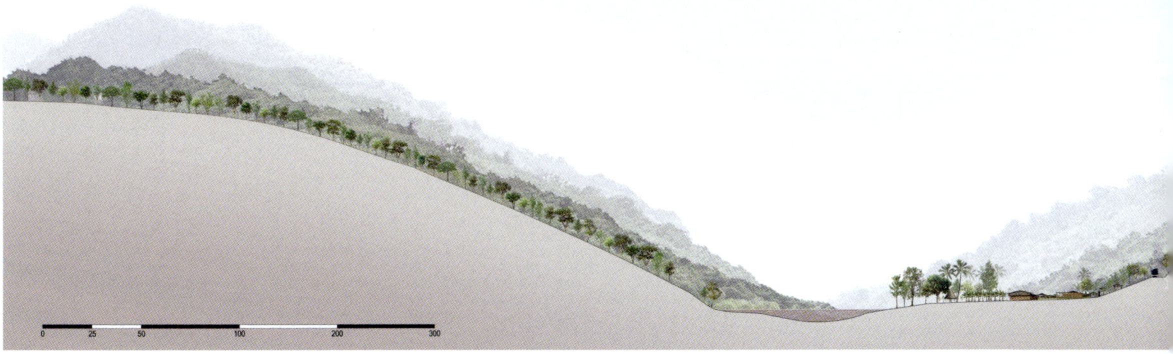

(FIGS. 2–9)
Eight cross-sections across the mestizo communities of Flores del Río Mayo, San Antonio del Río Mayo and Churuyacu del Río Mayo, as

(FIG. 10)
Waman samanas along the Atlas Río Mayo, 2018

Alexia León is a Peruvian architect, educator, and urbanist. She founded Lima-based leonmarcial arquitectos with Lucho Marcial in 2012. In 2021 the studio participated in the 17th International Architecture Exhibition—La Biennale de Venezia. She is co-curator, with Lucho Marcial, of the Peruvian pavilion at the 18th International Architecture Exhibition—La Biennale di Venezia. Her architectural and urbanism practice integrates her research on territory and landscape in the Andean Amazon, San Martín, Peru. The studio is itself an open platform that seeks ways to boost the design process through transversal conversations on structure, space, and materiality through prototype development, a process that analyzes not only the possibilities of what can be built, but also sparks the question of what can be built now, responsibly, and thinking of the common good.

How to Love a Tree (a Lament)

(10 min read)

Bara Gali
34.10000°N, 73.35000°E

Hira Nabi

During walks in the forest from 2019–2022, I kept encountering young trees that were already dead or slowly drying surrounded by other healthy trees. I puzzled as to what could be the cause of this. A fatal disease? Bad luck? A specific kind of rot? I began to look for answers, and found more questions by the end.

In the aftermath of heavy floods in Pakistan during the 1990s, all commercial activities in the forest were banned. After 2001, a policy was instated permitting the removal of "dead, dry, and diseased" trees for local villagers to use as firewood. This created an allowance for a dead tree to be logged. In the face of this logic, driven by biting cold winters, a last recourse to survival would be wagered. Residents from nearby towns would take axes to the trunk of a living tree, stripping off bits of bark from its trunk, cutting off the movement of vital nutrients so as to starve, and dry out the tree, and inevitably kill it. Once the tree started to dry out and die, it could be logged as a dead tree, as something legally removable.

There is a longer history to this as well, which must be offered for context. Colonial-era forestry practices sought to control the trees and forests demarcating the land as state-owned. The Indian Forest Act of 1878 "curtailed centuries-old customary use of communities over their forests, and consolidated the government's control over all forests… the use of the forests by villagers was abrogated, and then provisionally granted through concessions."[1] The colonial state made claims to the forest, and ensured their guarantee by use of violence, overriding the claims, rights, generational practices of forest dwellers, and the villagers in proximity to the forests. And the post-colonial national state continued with these codes and laws of extraction as management: a form of governance that paused only to update the dates on the legal contracts taking possession of the forests, rivers, mountains, and valleys.

1 Jisha Menon, *The Performance of Nationalism: India, Pakistan, and the Memory of Partition* (Cambridge: Cambridge University Press, 2012).

That policy of concession to local villagers no longer exists. Now, nothing can be taken from the forest, dead or alive. Yet, traces of that practice linger on, reminders of this act of antagonistic species survival.

I became interested in this phenomenon as I started to think of it as something more complex than the destruction of a tree. I recall, a few years ago, when I first heard of someone killing a tree: I recoiled in horror, and shock was palpable in waves across my body. Why would someone plot to kill a tree?

Over time, I have come to consider this while passing through several registers of pain, loss, and grief. First, I was made aware that a tree in a forest is never just a single tree. Trees inside forests and woodlands exist in communities. They dialogue, and communicate with one another, sharing resources, nutrients, warning each other of imminent danger, protecting one another, and living life together. Sometimes even after death. So the killing of a tree is an attack on a community of trees, on an entire eco-system of signals and generational passages, and ways of living.

The second thing I realized was that this is very different from acts of vandalism: of someone carving their initials into the trunk of a tree, or spray-painting graffiti across its bark, this is not a swaggering act of bravado. It isn't motivated to leave behind an imprint of your own selfhood on the world. This action was driven by desperation, and an urgent need to survive: to obtain fire-wood to cook food, and heat the house: to neither starve nor freeze, but to endure.

How can we imagine trees and woodlands as close kin? Can we imagine kinship so that it isn't just "tied to blood or family but extends to the land, water, and animals on whom we depend for livelihood?"[2] If kinship is about making something unknown familiar, perhaps we need to spend more time amongst

2 Andreas Chatzidakis, Jamie Hakim, Jo Littler, Catherine Rottenberg, and Lynne Segal, eds., *The Care Manifesto: The Politics of Interdependence* (London: Verso Books, 2020).

forests, to better understand trees, in their intimate habitats.

How is the pain of an axed, mutilated tree to be sensed?

On which scales can it be chronicled?

How does it compare with the misery of hypothermia or starvation?

Perhaps these are the mute, distressed signals of an impoverished landscape. Perhaps these are all laments that have come together to form an elegy.

Can I write about the desecration of a tree, and a forest in Murree without writing about inflation in Pakistan, and snowstorms that leave hundreds of people stranded and cut off?

I will try.

I spent two days with two trees, studying them closely: the arrival and departure of light became events that made visible to my eyes the grooves, indents, spider webs, lines of insects that moved and shape-shifted, deepened hues of reddish-brown bark, now turning muddy, now mahogany. I saw burnt bark that looked like cinder glistening beneath the midday sun, and I was permitted to glimpse pain, and life. Feeling the bark beneath the thin silken fabric that separated my hands from tree bark, even as they were busy over the trunk was a new way of learning its textures, its grain, and the splinters left behind by the encounter with the axe. I circled each tree, sat on the earth next to it, moved around its roots, felt the trunk beneath my fingers, gnarled, rough, unyielding and yielding, and as I pressed in, it left its imprints on my palms. The smooth parts were tricky, left behind by the axe; I could dislodge a splinter, and carry the violence with me, raw and chafed.

The trees passed on their encounters to me with a blunt axe, sharpened by need.

I leave you to imagine, and uncover the rest.

Hira Nabi is a Pakistani artist and filmmaker who uses her practice to think through vulnerable ecologies, extraction, conditions of labor, care, memories and hauntings, colonial legacies, modernity, and temporality. In her work, witnessing is an act charged with radical possibility, and one that holds immense potential for collective responsibility and love. *How To Love A Tree* (2019–ongoing) is a meditation on collapsing ecologies, gradual withdrawal, and the inevitable disappearance of worlds as multi-species environments. It is set in the towns and surrounding forests of Murree and the Galiyat, former colonial hill stations, in Pakistan. The work emerges from an intimate engagement with the environment, while also examining extraction as a through line between colonialism and modernity. She asks: "What does disappearance look like? What spectral traces does it leave behind? How can we care for one another as humans and beyond-human life forms?"

Reviving the Rural

(10 min read)

Songyang County
28.5305° N, 119.5321° E

Bishan Village
29.59999° N, 106.21666° E

Xu Tiantian in conversation
with Ou Ning

In 1978, the Chinese government introduced a series of major economic reforms that lifted millions from poverty. Forty-five years later, China is now not only the world's second-largest economy but has undergone a kind of transformation few countries have experienced, resulting in rapid and unprecedented urbanization that has left rural provinces and villages in a precarious place. This dynamic is central to the practice of architect Xu Tiantian. "While the disparity between rural and urban is global," she says, "the situation is even more urgent in China," where the populations of villages have dwindled. As founder of the Beijing-based office DnA_Design and Architecture, she has spent years working with traditional villages in Songyang to revitalize communities through what she describes as "architectural acupuncture." While these projects carry the potential for all kinds of frictions, they offer "a wonderful experience of mutual learning," says curator and artist Ou Ning, founder of Bishan Commune, a six-year rural reconstruction and community project. Speaking over WeChat, Xu Tiantian and Ou Ning shared their experiences of working in the Chinese countryside, from the daily challenges to the lasting impact of the rural.

Ou Ning Over the past decade you have built a body of work that in many ways sits at odds with the assumptions of globalization. More and more of the world's population is relocating to cities, but rather than taking on projects in urban areas, you have looked in the opposite direction to rural villages. Many of the projects designed by your Beijing-based office are sited almost one thousand miles south of that city, in Songyang County. What is it that made you want to create rural architecture, and what changes have you seen in Songyang?

Xu Tiantian The disparity between rural and urban is global—for example, I just returned from the village of Referinghausen in the Sauerland, a rural mountain range in the heart of Germany where I took students as part of the design studio I'm teaching at Yale (I would have loved to have taken them to China, but that was impossible due to travel restrictions). For many of these villages whose populations have left for cities, the challenge is how to attract younger people to live and work. The situation is even more urgent in China because so much focus has been placed on urbanization in major cities. This has resulted in regions that have lost significant amounts of their population. Many villages are known as "hollow villages," where only a few elders remain.

Over the past eight years our office has worked with Songyang County in Zhejian Province to restore its rural identity as well as stimulate circulation between local villages and the county urban center—we call this "Architectural Acupuncture." Through architectural intervention, a small-scale public program is introduced to each village and tailored to that village's local traditions and heritage. Drawing on the concept of acupuncture—a traditional part of Chinese medicine which takes a holistic view of the body and its energetic medians—architecture is seen as one element of a larger social structure that forms the village community. In our ongoing work, we discovered that more recently thousands of young people have returned to Songyang from major cities like Hangzhou or Shanghai. Many young families choose to live in the county's urban center and start new businesses in nearby rural villages, usually no more than an hour's drive away. Living in a county urban center and working in surrounding satellite villages is becoming a new mode of life. It allows a social infrastructure of education and health care for young families and at the same time provides new opportunities for startups on rural tourism and eco-agriculture in the nearby villages. It's more resilient and adaptive.

But you have also taught a course on the rural at Columbia University. I would love to learn how you bring your years of research and practice on rural into academia and education.

ON Rural and urban issues can be said to be different sides of the same coin. In my 2016 seminar at GSAPP, "City and Countryside in China," our work mainly focused on the mobility of populations, the change of geographical space, and the formation and evolution of the urban-rural dual structure during the most radical social changes in China in the past half century. Our studies revealed the political and economic driving forces behind these shifts, at historical and practical levels. Overall, the demographic changes in rural China are more shocking than those in Europe. Moreover, China's aging phenomenon is quite different from that of western countries. There is still a big difference between urban and rural areas in terms of employment, medical care, education, and other resources, which leads to a population that flows and centralizes in cities. As you said, young people leave the countryside to study or find jobs in cities. If they are unable to support their parents in the cities, their parents will stay in the villages, sometimes helping to raise the grandchildren, who are called "left-behind children." I lived and worked in a village in Anhui province for six years, and through this experience I learned that in order to bring young people back to the countryside and make repopulation possible, you cannot turn the countryside into a city; you have to create more opportunities for startups and employment in the countryside while trying to minimize the difference between the rural and urban in terms of working and living conditions.

(FIG. 1)
Bishan villagers help install an exhibition as part of Yixian International Photo Festival, 2012, photo Sun Yunfan

XT As you suggest, the goal of reviving these villages is not to make them more like cities but to restore their rural identities. Improved living conditions and the natural environment, alongside high-speed internet and modern infrastructure can attract young villagers to return home—and of course they would bring new resources and opportunities with their experience and knowledge from working in cities. The new market demands for rural cutural-tourism and eco-agriculture also bring huge income potential for these young people. They soon become pioneers in the new live-stream economy. In other words, the rural might not only provide alternative modes of living but also new types of revenue for rural economies.

ON How did your work in Songyang begin?

XT In the beginning we were commissioned to work on a different project in the county, which is still ongoing. During the first year (2014), wherever we went, whether visiting local tea plantations or ancient villages in the mountains, we were constantly asked for our design opinion or for advice on local village development. We ended up working on over a dozen small-scale pro-bono projects. It was a good learning process for us to understand local ways of building after collaborating with different village construction teams. These villages have been around for centuries, and each has something unique in its history and heritage. So we proposed a systematic collaboration within the county, adopting

Architectural Acupuncture as our methodology. It takes extensive research and communication—I call it the "diagnosis process"—to define a program, location, building scale, etc., before even starting on any architectural design. It was a "learning by doing" process, which started with projects related to village culture, history, and agriculture. Later, we moved onto rural regional infrastructure and facilities such as the Water Conservancy Center (2018) or Dushan Leisure Center (2019). We also applied acupuncture to urban neighborhoods where we found hidden histories and cultures. All these elements form a system that connects the county's urban center to its surrounding villages and rural areas.

The most difficult time was in the beginning, when locals were reluctant to collaborate. But after the first projects were built, more and more villages contacted us, and some even brought their own proposals. Our reason for working in rural environments is the people and seeing how the local community and village can change their perspectives and attitudes by experiencing the result and impact.

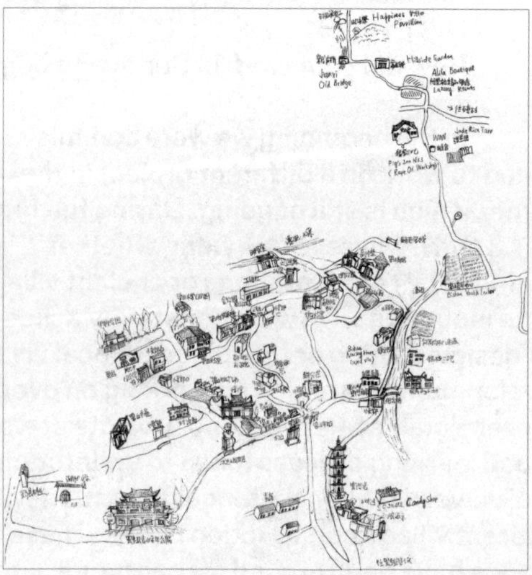

(FIG. 2)
Feng Zhiyin, map of Bishan Village, in the children's book *There Is a Village Named Bishan in China*, edited by Ou Ning, 2016 (unfinished)

ON The concept of Architectural Acupuncture seems to understand the rural society as a diseased body, and the architect as a healer who makes spatial diagnoses and provides therapy.

XT It's always a collective collaboration with the community and local authorities, involving many meetings and discussions. Our understanding of rural is about the depth of history and tradition in these places, and how people have lived there for centuries and generations. Those who work in local government are local people who grew up in these villages, who also have a strong sense of pride for their hometowns. The ownership and operations of all these architectural projects is also local—either by way of the village collective or township. I think this is essential. This type of collaboration is always full of difficulties and complications, and it is not always successful, but in those cases I wouldn't say that it is a total failure. In general, any good intention and innovation brought to a rural place will leave a trace of impact even if it goes unrealized.

ON The activism theory of anarchism calls this "propaganda of the deed"—that is, to prefigurate the ideals through direct action and mobilize people by way of the actual effects. I worked in this way in Bishan, a remote village located in the foothills of the Huang Mountains in Yi County, Anhui Province in East China, from 2011 to 2016. At the very beginning, the villagers didn't cherish their old houses but instead regarded them as a symbol of failure. As long as conditions allowed, they would build new houses and move, leaving their old houses behind. When an old house was sold to me cheaply, I made a simple renovation and moved in with my family from Beijing. The villagers understood that I cherished their architectural heritage and then started to realize the values of the property they had left behind. I had no problem getting along and communicating with the villagers—like you, I adhered to the principles of learning from one another and mutual respect. But because the Bishan Project (2011–16) (FIG. 1, 2) was not a commissioned project—it was, rather, a spontaneous experiment of rural reconstruction—it incurred a lot of frictions with the reality, especially when dealing with the authorities. At first, I always sought support from the government. They were initially enthusiastic, but as the Bishan Project became more impactful, officials became increasingly cautious until the project was actually banned by Beijing on the grounds that it was "out of the leadership of the Party." How as an architect do you navigate the desire to help these rural areas develop while maintaining your relationship with the government?

XT The acupuncture strategy is indeed a healing treatment targeting rural issues through collective collaboration between village communities, local governments, architects, local craftsmen, etc. The common symptom is that a village does not have confidence in its future. In general, the architectural intervention is meant to restore village identity, pride, and motivation. For example, the Wangjing Memorial Hall (2017) in Wang Village, named for one of the most important figures in Songyang history, an imperial scholar of the Ming Dynasty and the editor of the fifteenth-century Yongle Encyclopedia. The hall helped to restore a sense of history and pride among villagers. Another example is the renovation of the abandoned Shimen Bridge (2017), (FIG. 3) which once served as a main thoroughfare for a single village. Over time that single village was split into two: one on either side of the bridge. Rather than demolish the bridge, we proposed converting it into a viewing platform overlooking the Songyi River and the ancient Wuyang Dam. It now also reconnects the two villages. And in Xing, the new Brown Sugar Factory (2016) (FIG. 4) restores the community's unique brown sugar production as cultural heritage, while also upgrading the production quality. The factory integrates individual family workshops into one collective economic entity, ensuring a better performing rural economy.

Our architectural interventions in rural regions are not only about employing a certain vernacular, materials, or techniques. Rather,

(FIG. 3)
DnA_Design and Architecture, Shimen Bridge, Shimen Village, Songyang, 2018, photo Wang Ziling

they use a holistic approach that integrates the social and cultural with economic sustainability. As each village restores its own identity, the region eventually builds up a local social and economic circulation.

ON I saw a number of architectural projects when I visited Songyang in 2019. Not only yours, but buildings by architects including Wang Weijen, He Wei, Zhang Lei, and Liu Jiakun. The boom in this rural area is somehow reminiscent of the "Bilbao Effect" triggered by Frank Gehry's Guggenheim Museum and which through cultural investment and architecture reinvigorated the dying city. I saw many of your buildings including the poetic Bamboo Theater (2016), the Damushan teahouse (2015), and the Tofu Factory (2018) (FIG. 5) with the production process on show. The most attractive project was the Shimen Bridge. By covering the roof of the bridge, you turned a space for mobility into a place for pauses.

I was struck by the scale of some of the buildings. The Wangjing Memorial is large and good for the village, but the hall is still a very empty space. The Hakka Indenture Museum (2017) is large in scale, with very few pieces on display. I understood that architects have made many new spaces in Songyang, but it seemed that through the sorting, excavation, organization, and exhibition of local artifacts or objects there were still not enough to fill these spaces. There were also not many users when I visited, which left me with a feeling of "spatial surplus." What do you make of this situation?

XT I wonder how long you stayed in Songyang. If you only stayed for a few days to see all these new buildings, quickly running from one village to another, the experience could easily leave the impression you described. All these projects are small-scale buildings and make up a very small percentage compared to the overall building area in the entire county. More importantly, these buildings are serving a local community and village. This is exactly the opposite of the "Bilbao Effect," which involved an excessive investment in art and cultural institutions with little acknowledgment of local life or history. The acupunctural projects in Songyang County are undertaken with a limited budget, and they fully engage with their own place and people.

(FIG. 4)
DnA_Design and Architecture, Brown Sugar Factory, Xing Village, Songyang, 2016, photo Wang Ziling

It is ultimately ecological agriculture—not architecture—that is the main focus of Songyang County in its effort to revive rural regions. Many local agricultural plantations and producers of tea, rice, soya, and sugar cane have been upgraded. Villages have in turn started to revive their traditional festivals and ceremonies celebrating these products. For example, every November the Brown Sugar Factory becomes the stage for the Opening Sugar Festival marking the beginning of production. Even for us, as professional architects, the making of architecture is never the ultimate goal, but rather a means to revive the local culture. Traditionally each village only has had only one community space—the ancestor's hall—to accommodate various activities: weddings, funerals, festivals. This, of course, doesn't work with our current needs and activities. That's why these new buildings are multi-functional, designed not for exhibitions but rather for communing. Wangjin Memorial is articulated to free up space for gathering. The Hakka Indenture Museum is a popular pavilion on hot summer days. Damushan Teahouse is also an educational facility providing classes and certificates for tea ceremony. The Shimen Bridge is a spontaneous market place. All these projects are designed with intentionally low maintenance and operations as free, open spaces to help these villages achieve long-term self-sufficiency.

I find rural life fascinating because every region has its own pattern or heritage that is so unique. The local life patterns of rural public spaces are very different from cities. Things are much more spontaneous, based on weather and seasons, compared with the year-around scheduled public cultural programs of urban areas. In rural contexts the concept of public space can be much more flexible. This became the initiative for our Jinyun Quarry project (2021), (FIG. 6) an adaptive reuse of a cluster of abandoned quarries as various cultural and leisure spaces serving both the local community and visitors. Our current project (or subject), the adaptive reuse of abandoned Tulou buildings, also looks at disused spaces that have the potential to revive local heritage. Every time I visit Songyang, there's always something new. At the same time, our city life is becoming more or less the same everywhere. In recent years more and more young people are returning home from major cities, especially in the Yangtze River Delta area. In general working in a rural context required new perspectives, such as re-evaluating local resources, instead of implanting or super-imposing concepts from cities.

ON In Songyang, I saw that the Chenjiapu Bookstore designed by Zhang Lei was open for the public every day. The operator behind it is the Librairie Avant-Garde from Nanjing, which

(FIG. 5)
DnA_Design and Architecture, Tofu Factory, Caizhai Village, Songyang, 2018, photo Wang Ziling

(FIG. 6)
DnA_Design and Architecture, Jinyun Quarry, Songyang, 2021, photo Wang Ziling

I invited to open its first rural branch—the Bishan Bookstore—back in 2014. The Librairie Avant-Garde usually sends a store manager from Nanjing to take care of the daily business of each rural bookstore with two or three local employed villagers, and eventually its entire staff will be made up of locals. A rural bookstore can enter the village life through its daily operations, not just serving tourists. The full-time operation makes it possible for villagers to visit. This is how the Bishan Bookstore attracted villagers to participate in its activities: old people came to sit and read books, while children used its wi-fi to get online. If I had not been living in Bishan at the time—in other words, if I had only visited for a few days—I might not have seen these daily events. Just as my short trip in Songyang for two or three days, led to superficial impressions.

The "spatial surplus" that I felt in Songyang did not mean that the space created by architects exceeded the local building stock or population ratio, but that the excavation of historical and cultural resources, the activeness of local public life, and the incidence of daily cultural events seemed to lag behind the growth of these new spaces, thus leaving me with the "vacant" impression. But this rapidity of change can also cause conflict or frictions with locals, no? I read an article in *Time+Architecture* that mentioned the quarrel and reconciliation between you and a Mr Wang, a craftsman in Pingtian Village. Could you talk about what happened? How do you treat and deal with local craft and traditional construction technology?

XT The first time we met Mr Wang, he did not trust us at all. I think it had to do with multiple reasons. He did not trust that an outsider—especially a woman architect from the city—would understand local building traditions. As a construction master who normally works on important buildings like ancestors' halls, he did not believe that a

(FIG. 7)
DnA_Design and Architecture, Pingtian Village Center, Songyang, 2017, photo Wang Ziling

(FIG. 8)
DnA_Design and Architecture, Handicraft Workshop, Pingtian Village Center, Songyang, 2017, photo Wang Ziling

cluster of abandoned farmhouses at the entrance of Pingtian Village was worth renovating. (FIG. 7, 8) So from the outset he was reluctant about our project. There were a lot of debates and fights, even though the design interventions were minimal. Gradually, though, we saw that Mr Wang's attitude changed as he started to see the transformation of the original space. The building techniques were still local and traditional, but the adaptation of modern architectural elements, like continuity of space, courtyards, and skylights, totally changed the interior from small dark rooms into an open circulating communal space. He soon became actively engaged, providing knowledge and valuable construction experience. By the end, he was standing under the skylight and telling us that he wanted to build a similar house in his village.

The experience of working together was a learning process for us both. On the one hand, we needed to learn from those with local knowledge and resources. On the other hand, Mr Wang and local craftsmen began to understand and embrace modern concepts of architecture and space, which could transform the vernacular building typology into more adaptive public or community programs. More importantly, local villagers began to realize that, with architectural intervention, even the buildings in the worst condition have value and potential.

ON The restoration and reimagining of vernacular architecture also took place in Bishan, where I renovated old houses in the village to be used as event spaces. My own home was named Buffalo Institute. The Huizhou-style vernacular house from the late Qing Dynasty (early Republic of China) was open to the public as a venue throughout the day, and we also accepted volunteers to lodge in the house. The Bishan Bookstore and a later project, the School of Tillers (2015–2016), occupied former ancestral halls also built in the Huizhou-style. (FIG. 9) When renovating these old buildings, we reorganized and adjusted the interior spaces but never moved the supporting structures or altered their exterior appearance. It was important to reuse the bricks, tiles, and old wood purchased from the second-hand market and hire local artisans to work with us. In order to learn the local craft and traditional construction technologies,

(FIG. 9)
Bishan Bookstore, 2012, photo Matjaž Tančič

I asked three local villagers to help me build a tea pavilion with a special-shaped bamboo structure on a patch of reclaimed land. Because there was no electricity, everything was handmade. When drilling holes for the bamboo chips, the artisans showed me the amazing old drill that they pulled by rope. Several students from Tsinghua University and China Academy of Art joined us as volunteers. We worked in the wilderness like tribesmen or hippies who were interviewed by Lloyd Kahn in his publication *Shelter*. It was a wonderful experience of mutual learning.

Rural areas are also ideal fields for experimental architectural pedagogies, not only because students can study vernacular on site, but also because the context-oriented and socially conscious design practices in rural reconstruction projects are helpful in educating citizen architects. And as you know from teaching in Germany this term, rural areas everywhere have so much to teach us. In the 1990s Samuel Mockbee famously took his architecture students from Auburn University to the poor rural areas of western Alabama and later established Rural Studio to serve the local people. His students had the opportunity not only to learn about the reality and culture of rural America, but also to independently design and build projects by themselves—a much more meaningful experience than an internship in the city that would have been limited to research and drawing.

XT Isn't it fascinating when we really start to understand traditional architecture? The vernacular, often called "architecture without architects," is always a scientific, self-sustained system with local Indigenous wisdoms and a holistic approach with cultural and economic considerations. The making of a building involves collective collaborations that can also become intangible cultural heritage. In other words, the study and discussion of architecture in rural contexts should expand into more anthropological dimensions.

ON In this process of understanding and learning in a rural context, the deeper you go, the more you understand its rationality and splendor, and the more you are in awe of the order and beauty it presents.

Xu Tiantian is the founding principal of DnA _Design and Architecture and Professor in Practice at Tsinghua University. She has engaged extensively in the rural revitalizing process in China. Her groundbreaking "Architectural Acupuncture" is a holistic approach to the social and economic revitalization of rural China and has been selected by UN Habitat as the case study of Inspiring Practice on Urban-Rural Linkages. She is the recipient of numerous awards including the 2022 Swiss Architectural Award, the Global Award for Sustainable Architecture 2023, and the Berlin Art Prize / Kunstpreis Berlin–Architecture 2023. In 2020, she was appointed an Honorary Fellow of American Institute of Architects.

Ou Ning was chief curator of the Shenzhen & Hong Kong Bi-City Biennale of Urbanism/Architecture in 2009. In 2011, he founded the Bishan Project to join the rural reconstruction movement in China. From 2016–2017, he taught two courses, "City and Countryside in China" and "Curatorial Practice and Placemaking," at Columbia University Graduate School of Architecture, Planning, and Preservation. In 2020, he became the senior research fellow of the Center for Arts, Design, and Social Research in Boston. He lives and works in New York from 2022, and his most recent book is *Utopia in Practice: Bishan Project and Rural Reconstruction* (Palgrave Macmillan, 2020).

Moscow, a City of Mutual Silence

(10 min read)

Moscow
55.7461° N, 37.6177° E

Konstantin Kim

(FIG. 1)
Third inauguration of Vladimir Putin as president of Russia, May 7, 2012, Moscow

Even though we realize the hell that surrounds us, we cherish the contingency and possibilities of the moment. And we do believe in the sensuous world before us that will never disappear.

I

We meet outside in the freezing cold. After briefly speaking with a security guard, we are allowed inside, past a long queue of people so inadequately dressed you would never have known it was winter. It is December 2011, and I am sitting inside a nightclub called Gipsy, located on Moscow's exclusive "Golden Island." Across the table from me are two people: a high-ranking Gazprom official, who happens to be the father of the friends I'm with, and his friend—a Russian oligarch. What for my friend's dad began as an evening of "hanging out" with his son has turned into a lavish spending spree with unexpected companions coming and going, whispers and contacts exchanged with prolonged firm handshakes, wide smiles, and the kinds of misogynistic jokes that are shared only in the company of certain men. Few people can afford to have this kind of fun, but for those who can, a night on Golden Island, packed with exclusive establishments, affords the opportunity to both geographically and mentally detach from the otherwise agitated environment of Moscow.

Beyond the island's boundaries, the agitations are mounting. The Arab Spring has played out across Tunisia, Libya, Egypt, Yemen, Syria, and Bahrain, with hundreds of thousands participating in pro-democracy, anti-government protests. In Russia, opposition protests, stirred by the controversial 2011 legislative election, have continued for a year, while Dmitry Medvedev's first term as the third Russian president is coming to an end. Amidst it all, there is a feeling both of opportunity and indeterminacy. Which is why at some point in the evening I have decided to use this chance meeting with the oligarch to attempt to gain insight into something that for almost any Russian is inaccessible.

"Will Putin recede completely? And might Medvedev's era produce a path for a democratic Russia?" I ask him.

There is a slight pause and a brief discomfort in the air before the oligarch answers.

(FIG. 2)
Diller Scofidio + Renfro, Zaryadye Park, Moscow

"Have you read *The Prince* by Machiavelli?"

"No."

"Then do it. It has answers to the questions you ask."

Five months later, on the 6th of May, 2012, and 650 meters northeast from that nightclub, tens of thousands of people gather on Bolotnaya Square to protest what Russian and international journalists had reported on as a fraudulent presidential election. The protest ends with forceful dispersion, arrests, and prosecutions of civilians.

The next day, the newly elected President Vladimir Putin makes his inauguration cortege ride.(FIG. 1) His black Mercedes limousine, tailed by two black G-Wagons and surrounded by twelve black motorbikes driven by men wearing epaulettes, navigates the evacuated streets of Moscow towards the Kremlin. It is a spectacular appropriation of the city. Even more, it is a remarkable centralization of Putin's own identity—and, by proxy, a more general Russian identity. Driving through the empty streets that had been filled with thousands of protestors only the day before, this centripetal ritual marks a new era: an era when a once widely accepted outlook towards westernization is supplanted by notions of "Russia's special way" and "stability;" an era when the future began to be obfuscated by continuously revived glories of the past, and twenty-one years of inebriated clumsy liberation following the dissolution of the Soviet Union have turned into a withdrawal. Enter the "post-Soviet" condition.

II

The post-Soviet condition is shared by all of the former Soviet republics, but in Russia—starting in 2012 and rapidly transforming after the 2022 invasion of Ukraine—it has achieved a form of condensed time and space which has thickened, taken on flesh, and become artistically malleable.

The post-Soviet is a gray area. Coming out of the collapsed socialist realm, it has failed to integrate into the doctrine of late capitalism. It therefore occupies a liminal space between two grand disenchantments. Such a position is uncomfortable, but the alternative—that of integration—would mean first fully accepting the demise of the Soviet Union as a consequence of the failures of its own ideology and

(FIG. 3)
Strelka KB, the Pit (Yama), Moscow, now enclosed by a 1.5-meter-tall fence, ca. 2020

anti-humanist ways, and then repenting for those ways. But Russia is unable to process its past. A prominent spatial example of this denial is Lenin's mausoleum at the Red Square, which to this day hosts the unburied remains of the founder of Soviet Russia. A more systemic example is the continuous concealing by the Federal Security Service (FSB) of archives related to the period of the Great Purge—a suppression of information that is in direct contradiction with the 1992 presidential decree "On the removal of restrictive stamps from legislative and other acts that served as the basis for mass repression and attacks on human rights."

Post-Soviet Russia's inability to process both the past and its consequent failures and integrate into the future requires a coping mechanism: cynicism fills that need. A cynical position is an easy escape and a modus operandi of the post-Soviet. With a sly smile of "getting how things really are" it allows one to occupy a perceived moral high ground without accountability. Cynicism enables the post-Soviet to eliminate any imagined alternatives to itself, resulting in a condition that is ideologically bankrupt and solely reactive.

This reality manifests spatially. It is of no surprise that Moscow has seen its share of attention from renowned architecture firms: Herzog & de Meuron, Zaha Hadid Architects, OMA, Renzo Piano, MVRDV, and more have contributed to the Russian capital of today. A spatial post-Soviet exemplar is Zaryadye Park by Diller Scofidio + Renfro. (FIG. 2) Proposed by Vladimir Putin in 2012, the modest thirteen-hectare park occupies one of the oldest and historically significant raions adjacent to the Kremlin. It comprises an artificial hill, underground parking, a museum, concert hall, a cantilevering V-shaped bridge over the Moskva river, media center, restaurant, food hall, "ice cave" art installation with sub-zero temperatures year round, hotel-apartment, amphitheater semi-covered with a climatically controlled glass dome, and even vegetation in between. Zaryadye is a vanguard of a post-Soviet public space, a place so saturated with program that it leaves no space for self-expression and therefore, while allowing one to be in public, leaves no space for publicness. This is a necessary feature of the post-Soviet public space: to reduce publicness and contain contradictions.

In rare cases when the post-Soviet space is not prescribed and allows room for expression, it can sometimes result in its own subversion. Conflicts arise. The urban amphitheater at Khokhlovskaya Square, known colloquially as the Pit (Yama), was opened in 2017.(FIG. 3) Designed by Strelka KB, an urban development consulting company and affiliate of Strelka Institute, the space is an open, semicircular seating area cascading from ground level down to a spacious stage with an excavated, sixteenth-century wall foundation serving as a skene. Such casual museumification allowed for myriad publicness: young people playing chess, dancing, skateboarding, and playing frisbee while older generations enjoyed the vibrancy and observed the ancient centerpiece. The popularity of the project spoke of "well-crafted placemaking." At night, however, the Pit transformed into a venue for loitering, prohibited public drinking, loud music, antisocial behavior, and sexual activities. Recurring conflicts led to altercations with the police. Rather than confronting any number of reasons or symptoms that led to its malfunctions—such as overly restrictive laws on public drinking, a general acceptance of acts of intolerance and aggression, or police brutality—the contradictions were quietly swept under the rug, and in 2020 the Pit was quietly enclosed by a fence 1.5 meters in height with two easily policed entrances. The "Pit," together with publicness, brought up inner contradictions and a deeply atomized state of Muscovites: locals vs non-locals, young vs old, rowdies vs purists, police vs everyone.

It is July 2, 2016, and I stand among a large group of people, dressed predominantly in black, on the sidewalk opposite MoZAL, a Moscow-based machine-tool factory. MoZAL shut down in 2010 and has since rented out its facilities for various needs. For several weeks, more than one hundred people have been transforming the complex into a setting for a three-day techno festival that will host thousands of visitors. But the festival never happened. A group of men dressed in civilian clothes arrived with the police and forced everyone to vacate the premises, leaving behind tools, documents, and unfinished work.

A lot of theories are hypothesized on the sidewalk that day. Perhaps the festival sponsors have been caught laundering money—or they have not been laundering enough. Or maybe the high-ranking police officials never received their proper cut for looking the other way and ignoring potential drug consumption (par for the course at this kind of event). Or is it because techno culture does not ideologically fit into the Russian context—and therefore a crackdown is a part of a broader cultural policy. Meanwhile a young man, an artist, with a pale face and tired eyes smokes a cigarette as he looks across the road towards the previously blank wall of an administrative building which he has overpainted with a monumental unfinished mural.(FIG. 4)

We linger on the sidewalk for about an hour before somebody calls a cab and we drive away. In the moment, receiving no clear explanation seemed normal since all the sidewalk theories made sense all together and it made no difference which one was factual. The general fact was that at this point in time a certain amount of contradictions related to the festival became too big to be handled by patrons or the municipality or the police, and therefore work and expectations had to be quietly sacrificed to an undefined status quo.

The status quo is the post-Soviet's most desirable condition, a perfect instantiation of proclaimed stability. To preserve this status and the post-Soviet itself, a container is required, i.e., an identity. An ideology will not work due to the cynical coping mechanism. And nostalgia can only take you so far because the past cannot enchant and incorporate everyone due to the breakneck speed of the global.

If to some, identity comes historically prefabricated as pieces of a Crystal Palace to build and harmoniously cohabit, it is the cynical coping mechanism of the post-Soviet, standing on top of collapsed Soviet ruins, that would make a rude gesture to that palace. This is not a new condition for Russia. In 1864

(FIG. 4)
MoZAL factory, Moscow, 2016

Dostoevsky published *Notes from the Underground*, written three years after the emancipation reform that abolished serfdom, as a riposte to Nikolay Chernyshevsky's highly ideological *What Is to Be Done?*, a novel that imagines a utopia based on rational laws of self-interest. Dostoevsky's Underground Man—a lowly government worker—is critical towards rationalism or dogma of any kind. At the same time, through the rejection of that dogma, he is socially deprived and alone, forced further underground, and left to understand his identity only by way of what he is not. *Notes from the Underground* provides the blueprint for the kinds of problems that modern Russia produced and now chooses to ignore. Through a similar negation lies the identity of the post-Soviet, whose quest for identity turned out to be apophatic, or in other words, what that identity is *not* rather than what it is, concerned not with its own "thisness" but its "otherness." The Golden Island, for instance, with its lavish establishments, does not ignore a general social context of scarcity but openly negates it and therefore forms itself. Likewise, Putin's cortege—and by extension his government—does not establish itself by riding through Moscow's streets but by symbolically evacuating civilians, negating both their claims and their very existence.

Dostoevsky was producing art that rejected the dogma of his time (especially the ideas of the rational egoist), but in today's Russia, in order for any kind of cultural production to occur, there must be an acceptance of the post-Soviet condition. Consequently, a critical stance towards the post-Soviet cannot acquire a critical mass of supporters and in some cases risks compromising itself.

In 2017, Moscow initiated a fifteen-year program to renovate its Soviet-era housing blocks. More than five thousand buildings, mainly from Khrushchev's time (aka *Khrushchyovkas*), were to be torn down and replaced with new buildings. Critics and preservation communities have voiced concerns with the fact that buildings to be renovated were located in central raions with high land value. On top of this, the raions themselves risked losing up to 25% of vegetation and becoming 3.3 times denser, outcomes that would contribute to further congestion in an already overpopulated city. As the project was starting, I was asked to help out as a cameraman at a performance of a young woman I knew. Arriving at the agreed place in Basmanny District, I noticed about twenty young people standing in front of an old building. I was told that the building was to be demolished due to the renovation project. The performance consisted of hanging casts of the young woman's breasts on the building as charms to represent a form of protection and care for the homes of those to be evicted and relocated.

I filmed the building, the artist's casts, and an interview, as well as the young men and women clapping in support of the performance, and the delighted grandmotherly reactions of three old ladies who proclaimed their gratefulness to the young woman and their hopes to live in the house for many years. When, after the shoot I asked about the old ladies, I was told they were hired actresses. But the unease I felt, brought up by the questionable ethics of such spectacle, could not be voiced. The performance was highly covered in Moscow news. Sometime later, the young woman had a successful political campaign and became the municipal deputy of Moscow. She was forced to flee Russia in 2022 due to political prosecutions for her anti-war pronouncements on social media. In the meantime, the building was quietly demolished.

III

What drives cultural production if all notions or visions of change have been evacuated from the public realm and corrupted by the post-Soviet condition? In 1991 Viktor Misiano published an article, "Cultural Contradictions of *Tusovka*," in which he tried to define a mutated social organization of artists as culture producers, which had been forming around time of the dissolution of the USSR. He named that form *tusovka*, a Russian term for a gathering of people with no particular purpose other than socializing. He describes:

> *a form of self-organization of the artistic environment that is chronically lacking in state support. ... It came about as a direct result of the breakdown of official culture and its institutions. ... A distinctive characteristic trait of* tusovka *is its bringing together of a number of people that are otherwise not organized in concrete structures—whether institutional or ideological—but only through the prospect of their gain.* Tusovka *considers itself as pure potentiality; it is an artistic social project.*

In this context, those who chose to resist the condition went underground and have therefore accepted precarious obscurity. Those who accepted the condition in their culture production, knowingly or not, formed a peculiar entity the post-Soviet allowed: that of the *tusovka*. *Tusovka* persevered and eventually rooted itself in the gray area of the post-Soviet— that field saturated with an ethical ambiguity and easy money, a lack of publicness and institutional engagement and therefore a lack of grounds for a critical discourse. All of the above factors and others have turned most prominent *tusovka* members into prophets with state support and official titles while others have become owners of boutique galleries, restaurants, bars, clubs, or publishing houses. In a condition where social change is not possible, one's creativity tends to find its release in entrepreneurship. Cultural projects of *tusovka*, for the most part, were neutral in relation to the post-Soviet. And yet the by-product of these projects is always a contextualization and spatialization of the post-Soviet condition. *Tusovka* was spatial because it was precarious and demanded physical filtering for its own preservation: thresholds, passages, rituals, face controls, dress codes, etc. Members of *tusovka* detached from the public and constructed heterotopias. In a city where it is easy to be in public as long as you behave accordingly, they strived to create spaces that provided a sense of belonging and a refuge.

A DIY techno club called Rabitsa organized by Moscow DJs and artists was

(FIG. 5)
OMA, Garage Museum of Contemporary Art (2008), 2017, Garage Museum for the GLAM WIKI project

strategically positioned in an unknown, triple-gated industrial area of an "Aviator" factory with no signs or advertisements. A narrow inner courtyard covered with pallets and up-cycled furniture united old garage spaces on its perimeter, which were remodeled into stages. This small venue hosted world-renowned musicians and became a cultural hub and a safe space for Moscow's oft-persecuted LGBTQ+ community—until it was raided a year after its opening by OMON in tandem with aggressive people in civilian clothes. Two weeks after the incident, club owners released a statement of an indefinite closure of Rabitsa with no comment.

Chaotic *tusovka* has been the predominant artistic environment in Russia for more than twenty years. And thirty years after Misiano's article, I want to add that although it is obvious that *tusovka* has had its way, it may now have ultimately run its course. In Moscow, following the overly abundant 2000s, new forms of cultural institutions, funded mostly by oligarchic money and propagated by *tusovka* members, began to emerge: Garage Museum, Strelka Institute, VAC foundation, to name a few (with the headquarters of the latter two organizations strategically positioned on the Golden Island). Through their influence these institutions have reclaimed the cultural production from a romanticized secrecy and made it public again. With their power they have "domesticated" some members of *tusovka* enough to recontextualize culture from something to be presented to the masses to something produced with them.

Garage Foundation, co-founded by Dasha Zhukova and Roman Abramovich, a Russian oligarch currently sanctioned by the EU and UK over his ties with Vladimir Putin, opened a museum of contemporary art in Gorky Park in 2015. (FIG. 5) The OMA-designed building consists of a rectangular polycarbonate envelope that encloses the structural remains of Vremena Goda, a café built in 1968, preserving a palimpsest of colorful mosaics, murals, and graffiti. (FIG. 6) The café's existing horizontality of slabs was broken up by ramps, stairs, and volumes evoking Moisei Ginzburg's concept of a social condenser whereby varying programs are layered or partially superimposed on a space to create intentional collisions and in turn a questioning of programmatic hierarchies within the space and the social

(FIG. 6)
Igor Vinogradsky, Vremena Goda Cafe, 1968, now the site of the Garage Museum, Moscow, Garage Museum of Contemporary Art

hierarchies that form them. Although the spatial organization together with museum's liberal policies were able to evoke novel productive forms of publicness, ultimately they did not risk questioning the post-Soviet as the main driver for existing social hierarchies. Any potential created by the condenser ended up being contained and extinguished by the neutralizing translucent polycarbonate envelope. Garage Museum together with other new cultural institutions in Moscow did not become public platforms for the cross-examination of broader power structures.
In this sense they became bigger, more accessible heterotopias—islands of their own publicness limited by their very boundaries.

Epilogue

Since the start of the war in Ukraine in February 2022, the number of people who have fled Russia is approaching one million. My friends and colleagues have found refuge in Georgia, Turkey, Kazakhstan, Armenia, Uzbekistan, Germany, Austria, Bulgaria, and Cyprus. Currently and, I am afraid, even when the dust of the war settles, we all face returning to a country with far less gray area and a more merciless nature than the post-Soviet. Some of us will choose not to go back.
But even if we cannot reclaim our physical space within Russia, it would be a missed opportunity not to reclaim a sense of trust and belonging among ourselves. Whether inside or outside of Russia, we as Russian producers of culture have redemptive work to do. This work will be pointless or even harmful if we don't process and leave behind the post-Soviet condition that weighs us down. We must face a kind of death-rebirth cycle, a repentance that I see as a therapeutic endeavor, and one that is made easier if shared. Because—and this is the crux of the matter—the post-Soviet condition exists within each of us. I propose

taking a more conscious path of self-healing through collective proactiveness, rather than one that simply reacts to the current obvious reasons for our precarity.

Although we are stripped of ways of being in public together we should not relinquish our publicness, a resource to be cherished and shared. It is heartfelt forms of publicness to which the post-Soviet is intrinsically allergic. And these new forms of publicness, which we can invent together, will help to reestablish our mutual trust. The outcome could become a robust supportive creative network, inevitably seeping back into our country. Our common project could become an alternative Russia, one which is de-territorialized by us, one which needs our creative inputs now and resists being indulged by the powers that be or the powers that will be.

There are many questions we must ask ourselves: questions of open disagreements and public discussions, questions of the social responsibility of our crafts, questions of institutional engagements within and outside of our country, new institutions and their support, oligarchic money, and compromises. We should be ready to bear responsibilities for these and their answers.

Until those uncomfortable questions become parts of our publicness—instead of being quietly swept under the rug—we will still stand with one foot in the post-Soviet, unable to regain our creative integrity. We will keep feeling marginalized and alienated, cherishing our uniqueness "underground." If, however, by working through those questions we acquired the skills to temporarily surrender our preciously preserved but ultimately brittle identities, we could pave a way out of the post-Soviet condition, a way out for each of us and all together. And in our astounding city or elsewhere we might find out that we already belong, and we always have.

To all that has run its course, and to the vast unsayable numbers of beings abounding in Nature, add yourself gladly, and cancel the cost.
— Rainer Maria Rilke
"Sonnets to Orpheus"

Konstantin Kim is a Moscow-born architect, writer, and political activist. His interests lie in understanding the developments of architectural languages and forms of production of architecture as processes of liberation. His current research analyzes the work of architecture groups through a lens of solidarity, in particular Soviet avant-garde groups and fascist rationalist groups of the 1920s and 1930s, and traces transformations of architects' solidarity in tandem with works through Stalinism in the USSR and the decline of fascism in Italy into Soviet modernism and postwar Italian architecture. In 2020, together with KaWai Cheung and Aleksa Milojevi he co-founded, *Half-circus*, a traveling architectural assemblage that operates between Europe, Russia, and the US.

Diary of an Accumulation

(12 min read)

London
51.5183° N
0.1308° W

Vienna
48.2017° N
16.3652° E

New York
40.8075° N
73.9626° W

Hong Kong
22.2841° N
114.1378° E

Ithaca
42.4534° N
76.4735° W

Paris
48.8567° N
2.3336° E

Nasrine Seraji

Leonard da Vinci, detail of friction studies, from Codex Arundel, British Library, London (Arundel folio 41r c. 1500–05)

One of Boyarsky's recommendations to a young AA student

The word friction is familiar to most of us because it provides us with one of the first lessons in physics. Friction in architecture, however, is a very different story and a necessary condition for critical thinking and analytical debate.

We know that figures such as Aristotle, Vitruvius, and not least Leonardo da Vinci—the first person to record the laws of friction in 1493—all maintained a somewhat promiscuous relationship with architecture. Still, today—despite the fact that Vitruvius himself published the discipline's first-ever treatise—most are recognized as mathematicians, theorists, or engineers, never as architects.

But how can someone who identifies as an architect—a person who has simultaneously taught and practiced architecture, a condition that is its own kind of sliding friction à la Leonardo—design a pedagogical method that contributes to the topic? The answer is not as clear-cut as the drawings in Leonardo's notebook. Or rather, it isn't as evident from the outset. Instead, it seems that the frictions an architect experiences—as a student, designer, practitioner, and teacher—are cumulative. If you are aware of one friction, others may only seem to be background noise. And it seems that only with the benefit of hindsight you can see which surfaces were rubbing against one another.

Friction 1
1977
School / School

August 1978, the Architectural Association School of Architecture, 36 Bedford Square, London. A meeting between A. G. Seraji (my father) and Alvin Boyarsky, the most emblematic chairman of the AA. "What should Nasrine read before she starts?" asked my father with me in earshot, as if I was still in primary school. Alvin's response: he could give me a list of books to read before school starts, but only if it was my request and not my dad's. Welcome to a new meaning of school: autonomy, will, and independence. I still remember on the famous list (yes, I went back and asked for it myself): Walter Benjamin's essay "The Work of Art in the Age of Mechanical Reproduction," *The Poetics of Space*, by Gaston Bachelard, and the *Architecture of the Well-Tempered Environment*, by Reyner Banham.

Friction 2
1980
Wildness/Taming

The AA had the most wildly fantastic parties, or at least this was its reputation. In 1980, while I was in my third year, the school held a Bal Masque in the style of the Beaux-Arts and Bauhaus. The theme was "Taming"—a play, it turns out, on "Mating," which we could actually get away with calling it. The students came up

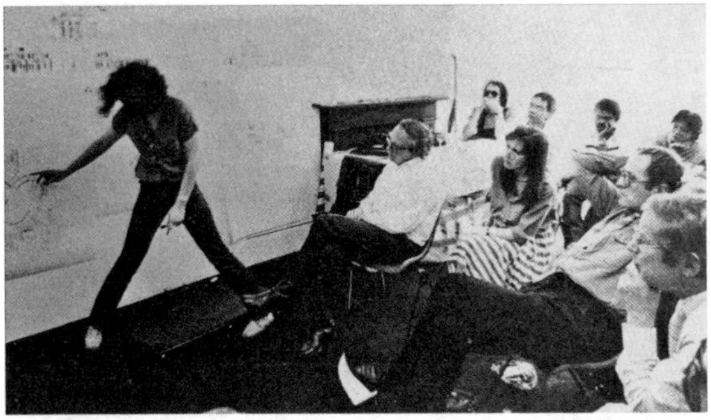

AA Diploma unit with Peter Cook, Christine Hawley, Warren Chalk, and Bob Maxwell

"As a woman I have no country, as a woman my country is the world of architecture."

with the most incredible costumes: Clark Gable and his pet Puma, Dracula (me) and his bride, and the American werewolf in London (one of our tutors). On reflection, we were perhaps projecting the fantasy relationship we wanted to have with our future clients, believing that an imagined situation could be the origin of another reality. And indeed, at the AA we never thought of architecture as a profession. It was always a discipline and a craft that would lead us to a profession (or client) of our choice depending on how we appropriated our own educations. We were wild but there was a precise elegance and carefulness in the way we had designed and disguised our tamely natures.

Friction 3
1982
Choice/Freedom

October 1982, central staircase of the famous Georgian house at 36 Bedford Square.

Alvin Boyarsky: "So what have you decided? If you are going to Zaha's diploma unit, I would not like to hear two women arguing in this staircase."

Me: "Well, the choice is between Zaha and the two Peters (Wilson and Cook). But Zaha still doesn't know what we'll be doing, and Peter Wilson is only interested in us drawing as beautifully as he does."

I had no choice but to join Peter Cook, Christine Hawley, and Jeremy Dixon in their "Super Unit" of thirty-six students. They promised us total independence, the ideal refuge. That freedom even determined the final project. When ten of us could not afford the unit trip to the US or secure a visa, we chose an alternative site in the UK: Scarborough, in the north of England. The forgotten 1930s resort town demanded of us as architects to be more political and more socially conscious of environments that had once enjoyed a glorious past and needed fresh ideas to be transformed.

Friction 4
1983
Melancholy/Nostalgia

I graduated in the summer of 1983 and on July 2, we went to celebrate our not-yet-confirmed diplomas at the Milton Keynes Bowl where David Bowie and his incredible yellow suit shined among millions of spectators. The performance still plays vividly in my memory, as well as the day after: the Post-Diploma Trauma (PDT) had settled in. What was I to do? Where was I to go? Most of my fellow graduates were returning to their respective countries of origin: Japan, the US, Hong

Kong, etc., to work as architects. I had not been home to Iran since 1979, and I knew that it would be very difficult or even impossible for a woman to return and work in the country as an architect. The risks of not being able to travel freely were being propagated. On the one hand I felt that I no longer had a country to return to; Iran had become an Islamic Republic. On the other hand, it was exciting to see what the changes were. Most importantly all references (books, architecture, art, etc.) to Persia and the culture of my country of birth were being put into question. If these ideas weren't destroyed, they were placed in captivity.

I felt exile was now my default condition. I would always be an outsider, not only in my own country (as a woman and liberal) but also in the UK and later in France, my eventual home. I was forced to construct an imaginary country for myself. With some help from Virginia Woolf, I determined my path: "As a woman I have no country, as a woman my country is the world of architecture." I have often asked myself whether this was a form of nostalgia? Or perhaps I was entering a deep melancholic state from which to construct my new future. The difference between nostalgia and melancholy is that the former is romantic and debilitating, whereas the latter is constructive and thoughtful. Born in Tehran, educated in London, cultivated and politicized in Paris. I see it now: what a privilege to always be the one in the margins and never at the center, always at ease, with a home that is everywhere and nowhere.

Friction 5
1985
Academia/Practice

Two years of working in the best-paying offices with absolutely no design thinking—in fact no thinking at all: it made me wonder, why we were taught to think in schools? The AA had saturated us with all that mattered, which was to think and to be critical. To look at the world analytically, and to never settle for the

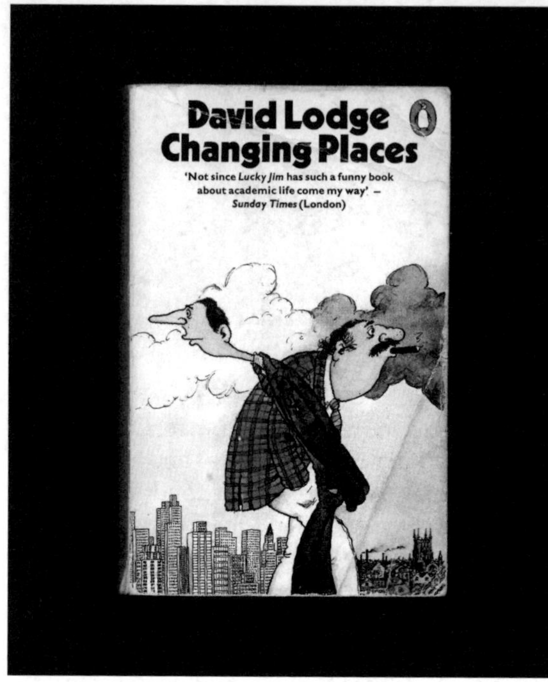

"A parody of academic culture on the two sides of the Atlantic."

status quo. In commercial offices the time sheet (and how one filled theirs) was more important than how one thought.

No time to think. Deliverables are the only necessity in order for the office to bill the client in a timely fashion. And Fridays are pub nights where there is a sense of belonging to the same group of people who are contributing to forming the planet as God's Junkyard.

Friction 6
1996
Ivy League/Other Schools

The fees are one hundred times more expensive than public European schools. What is it that the students learn at an Ivy League that is worth that? Not much more, in fact. So where do the fees go? With the exception of a few Pritzker winners, the other tutors are not lavishly paid either. Is studying with a top-notch architect one day per month enough to make it worth joining the Ivy club? By the mere fact of limiting the acquiring of knowledge and experience through high-profile architects to a few schools, we have created a tiered profession, no longer a discipline. Having been tutored by a famous architect becomes a line on the CV, as if academia had swapped places with the world of practice.

Early in my teaching career I held posts at Columbia and the AA simultaneously (both elite schools). I arranged for the AA students to come to New York and the students from New York to go to London. The topic of the studio was the renovation of the cities' respective meat markets. For the final reviews we asked the students to present one another's projects and not their own. This created the most incredible sense of detachment. It enabled each student to defend the work of one another and to understand how to distance themselves enough to speak critically. Perhaps the idea of comparison came to me on those flights back and forth as I read *Changing Places*, by David Lodge, a parody of academic culture on the two sides of the Atlantic. It was important for the students in the early 1990s to understand the structure and specificity of their learning environments and acquire the ability to self-evaluate.

It is time to translate Scharoun's idea of the vineyard in his Berlin Philharmonic hall to architectural education. The players and the audience can be in constant dialogue and make architecture conduct.

Friction 7
2001
Architecture/Symbol

911 was known to the French, the English, and the Americans as Nine-One-One (the emergency phone number) until September 11, 2001 when it changed to Nine-Eleven. The architecture of the twin towers rumbled in an hour, a building that had taken fourteen years to build. Architecture is slow.

September 11, 2001, 9am. My first meeting at the department of architecture at Cornell was interrupted by a scream from down the hall. The first plane had struck the tallest symbol of capitalism. Architecture would never be the same. A new chapter of history was scrolling across all the TV screens around the world. A friend told me that shortly after, she had bought a large screen to follow the events in their full spectacle; the society of spectacle was being rolled out before our eyes. My mother had called my hotel in Ithaca (run by the Hotel Management School at Cornell), and they mistakenly told her that I had checked out. I had simply lost myself in the midst of it all, watching all the news channels: NBC, BBC, CBS, FOX, France 24, CNN, all from the comfort of my hotel room overlooking the belltower of Cornell University. It was an exercise of critical analysis, comparing the degree of hatred and animosity for the act based on the political colors of each broadcasting house. From that day on, the press was no longer neutral.

It was an incredible introduction to what could happen if or when the Gulf Stream collapses. The towers were the absolute symbol of "dollar power" and the belief in structural integrity and ingenuity. They were, with their imposing volume, the symbolic gateway to New York, the city where Rem Koolhaas wrote his retroactive manifesto *Delirious New York* (having spent some time in Ithaca at Cornell with O. M. Ungers): New York, New York, that twentieth-century metropolis where architecture is both a fiction and a symbol.

But while history had changed, architecture and its education didn't. Form, however, became much more important than content. I couldn't help but think of the explosion of the Pruitt-Igoe apartments by the same architect some thirty years previously. If that was, as Charles Jencks claimed, the end of modern architecture, where were we now?

Friction 8
2006
Privilege/Face recognition

Between 1996 and 2001, I had the opportunity to be the first foreign woman under the age of forty to head one of the two *Meisterschule* at the Academy of Fine Arts Vienna. The *Rektor* was an architect, Carl Pruscha, who had renovated the famous Semperdepot, designed by Gottfried Semper and built a few years before his death in 1879. It is still one of the most amazing spaces (originally conceived for the hanging of theater sets) to exhibit art and architecture. This alone made me extremely excited to take up the offer to head the *Meisterschule* that Gustav Peichl had directed for twenty-three years (1973–1996). Tradition demanded that I meet with him in the famous Café Sacher where he could pass on the keys (plus the special key to a lavatory that only the *Meister* could use).

It was an absolutely comical hazing ceremony that repeated itself, albeit in a more extreme form in 2002, this time led by the students of Cornell University's architecture department. They took me to dinner and then to a bar (a strip club) and called the Chair of Architecture (me) up on stage. The brain had to work in an instant. I had to somehow be cool while respecting university by-laws and discretions. That's where a winter hood came in handy. Pulled up over my face, there was no fear of being recognized in the morning paper. More than twenty years later, I still wonder why this ceremony was so important to the American students. Was it really to bond with their new Chair of department? Or was it to make sure I knew that in a school, the students hold the power.

Friction 9
2012
East/West

After positions in the US and Europe, I wanted to know whether it was possible to have a different experience as head of the architecture school at Hong Kong University. With a strategic position in southeast Asia that was long under British rule, Hong Kong is a banking society that maintains a privileged relationship to the West. This juxtaposition of history and culture allows the city to function as a pivotal marker and platform for experimentation with alternative infrastructures, forms of living, making, and fabricating. And until recently, in contrast with mainland China, it held a starkly different relationship with media, arts, and politics. So why had the ex-dean of HKU, Ralph Lerner, promised to make the school the Harvard GSD of Asia?

I was much more interested in inscribing HKU architecture as a unique golden peg on the map of Asia. Why couldn't the school create a consortium of very good schools in relatively close proximity: India, Sri Lanka, Singapore, Taiwan, Thailand, the Philippines (what I had called the five-hour circle of influence), as opposed to bilateral conventions with the US and Europe? These territories and China make up more than half of the world's population, and their architectural questions are diametrically different and sometimes more urgent than those posed in Europe and America. Questions of infrastructure, landscape, and rapid rural disfiguration in the name of urban development were and still are fantastic opportunities for architecture schools to reinvent the future of Earth.

Friction 10
2018
The End/The Beginning

Universities used to be the haven of freedom and political resistance. This was not the case in Hong Kong. I had no choice but to step down from my post because I had shed light on some of the faculty's abuse of the system. I had also promoted the faculty members who taught more than the ones who were pretending to do so. And finally, I had to leave because I had dared to bring the school together to run a vertical project, formed of students in every year, called "Reclaiming Central." The program was an acknowledgment of Occupy Central (also known as the Umbrella Movement) of 2014, in which tens of thousands of activists (mainly students) occupied the city for seventy-nine days demanding more transparent elections and protesting China's interventionist policies. My hope was to reengage the public with their city which had been brought to a standstill in light of the protests. The University of Hong Kong is a public university, and I strongly believe that every public institution needs to engage with the taxpayers who fund it. Sadly, we never got that chance.

In June 2018, I left the school and took the plane to Paris in order to close the office and put an end to practicing experimental and critical architecture. Is leaving a school or closing an office truly the end, or is it a beginning of another chapter in engaging with education and speculating on architectural practices otherwise and elsewhere? Alvin Boyarsky used to say, "We are in pursuit of architecture, we discuss it boldly, we draw it as well as we can, and we exhibit it." He would have been asked to step down if he were teaching today. Universities no longer allow space for bold or frank discussions. While the canon and history of architecture are benefitting from courageous efforts to revisit the past and take stock, this should be a project of expansion, not erasure. In many schools of architecture, history is being rewritten by the hands and eyes of the politically correct. This is cowardice, and it is detrimental to the reality of how architects need to be educated: and that is with boldness, frankness, and even criticism. Where does this leave the next generation of students if the only knowledge they can access is a reformulated and decontextualized set of deformed realities?

Friction 11
2021
Democracy/Mob Power

January 6, 2021. The mob entered the US Capitol Building, destroying the archetypal house of democracy. Demolition is, to the optimist, the sign of something new to come. Architecture always starts with some form of demolition. Ironic that in order to construct a new idea, a new building, or a new "thing" we need to demolish the precedent. "Precedent" is a legal term which allows for a case to be examined in the context of a preceding example. Precedents in architecture can only be alibis, justifying the act of designing only in relationship to that which has already been done. Isn't it strange that although students are expected to make something new (adding to the book of knowledge of architecture), they are expected to justify their work through that which has come before?

The precedent is useful only if it is annihilated through critical analysis. I prefer to create a book of references for my students (not necessarily only from architecture, but coming from economics, arts, news, ecology, philosophy, sociology, etc...), enabling them to see the relationship and tensions between disciplines, because for architecture to survive, it must be able to have critical dialogues with all other disciplines. References allow for debate and analytical vision; precedents justify mob power.

Friction 12
2023
Past/Future

The Villa Savoye (1931) is nearing its one hundredth birthday. The house was the physical manifestation of Le Corbusier's five points of architecture, the blueprint of a lifetime pursuit. Every single house thereafter was based on the questions raised by the Villa. He even drew it at the tip of the branches of a tree-like organization, proposing that it would be the essence and perfect model of a house for the development of land in a variety of contexts. Even if it became synonymous with modern architecture, the Villa Savoye is also the epitome of a soured relationship between an architect and the client. In fact, it was never conceived as a normative house but as a manner in which one would live in the automobile century. It was always a thesis, a model of an idea: "The house as a machine for living."

By contrast, its alter ego, the Villa dall'Ava, is only thirty-two years old. Though it is geographically near the Villa Savoye, it follows a totally different set of preoccupations, a thesis as well but one that reveals many radical ideas of its architect, Rem Koolhaas. Here we can observe a prime example of an Oedipean relationship between two of the greatest architects of the twentieth century. All five points are revisited and reinterpreted by Koolhaas: the pilotis that look like the legs of a dancing giraffe; the strip windows that have a very different function than those of Corb's; the non-loadbearing facade is clad in a flimsy corrugated metal, as if to prove that it is non-loadbearing; the ramp and finally the roof terrace, where one finds the pool drawn toward the Eiffel tower, to show that the Villa is not in the city. The Villa dall'Ava is a great demonstration of cinematic sequences where its actors are the family and those (Dalí, Vermeer, and others even a few surrealists) who occupy the house. These elements also provide clues about the many discussions between the owners of the house and the architect as well as the architect and his influences in architecture. Here, it is seemingly a true love affair between the architect and clients.

How will architecture students talk about this house when it turns one hundred? Will they simply forget its relevance and its relationship to the other Villa? Will they think that the 90s were the years that one could think about architecture as an idea embedded in a discursive discipline and not a mere solution to the client's desires? Will architecture even survive the test of time? Perhaps architecture will have an energy rating label on it, just like all household appliances. Can architects be content with repairing as opposed to making new buildings from scratch? Repairing needs a knowledge of the "thing," its idea, and its function. But also, a politicized mind and a sense of altruism.

Perhaps the only way for architecture and its education to be relevant again is to unpack the past carefully and transform some fragments of it into the foundations of the future.

133

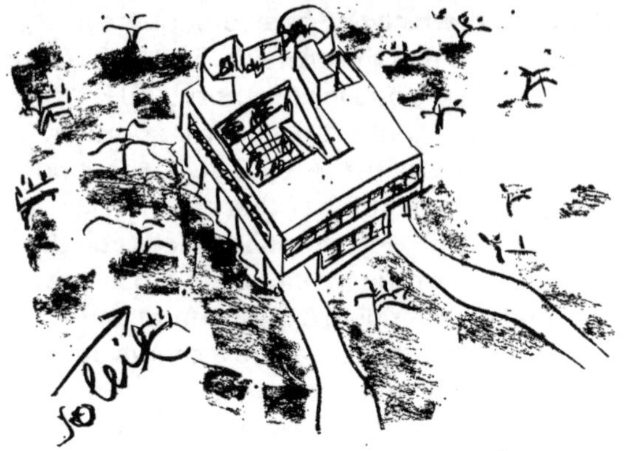

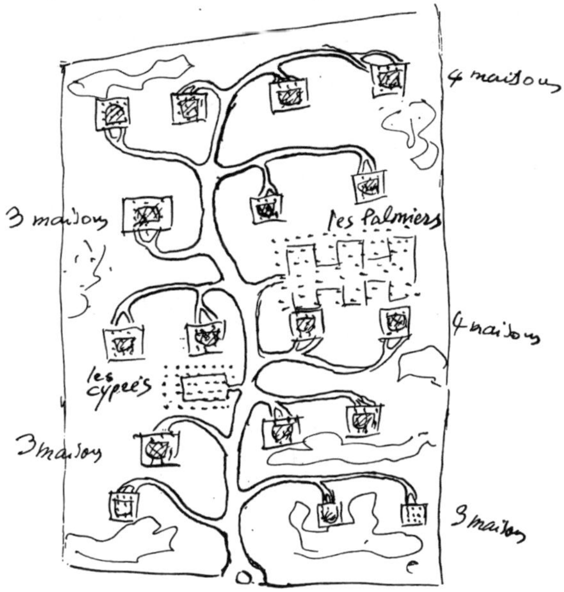

134

Le Corbusier, Villa Savoye as a tree of architecture, from *Precisions*, 1930 © FLC / Bildrecht, Vienna 2023

Nasrine Seraji is an architect and educator. After studying at the Architectural Association and practicing for a few years in London, she won the competition "Inventer 89" celebrating the bicentenary of the French revolution. This initiated her move to Paris and the formation of her studio where architecture was treated as both a cultural debate and a critical necessity. She is currently Professor of Architectural Design at University College Dublin and Distinguished Professor of Design and Research at Wenzhou Kean University. Her practice and research concentrates on housing and new models of urbanism. Her book and exhibition *Housing, Substance of our Cities* is a critical view on one hundred years of collective housing in Europe. She is in the process of writing a book on the discipline of architecture and education of architects and their overlap with practice.

When Walls Speak to Us

(12 min read)

Cañada Real, Madrid
40.33791° N, 3.58994° W

Santiago Cirugeda and
María Paz Núñez Martí

I am here, and you are there.
In front of my wall, we silence each other.
What are you looking at, what are you waiting for, what are you lo
Is my home different from yours, or my place more unusual than y
Are your needs different from mine? And is my family another kin
Perhaps you think that only a wall separates us, just a wall built w
Or maybe, just a wall... mirror of your gaze.
I wish it was just that, just a pile of bricks that you look at.
A broken grill.
A split tarpaulin.
... If only it were an open door, or better, a passage without a door.
If only it were an entry capable of connecting our lives.
Because in these walls is our history
They gather our life,
They express our feelings
They show our pain and our prayer.
With different tongues, in different languages, the fruit of our div
Whether Spanish, Portuguese, Romanian, or Moroccan.
With different creeds, Christian or Muslim.
These walls, canvases honored by your gaze, also receive and tat
I am here and you are there.
Looking at the present, uneasy because we do not know what fat
hoping for solutions that will facilitate and improve our quality of
Looking for resources of all kinds that will allow our children a qu
But I am still here. In Cañada, behind these walls.
Listening to your silence. Today, you are a spectator of a play in w
because we are poor, because we live in shacks, because it is very
know how to react, what to do... more than just stare at me.
I'm still here.
Listening to your silence.

for?

ople?
hands.

rigins.

r hope and our fears.

ts us because of our situation of legal irregularity,

f life, at least, similar to the rest of the people in the city...

ou do not act, accomplice of the generalized inaction,
to look at each other face to face and recognize that you don't

“Politicans Crooks.” Cañada Real Galiana is the largest and oldes
which is also the largest in Europe.

rmal settlement in the Autonomous Community of Madrid,

Eighty percent of Cañada's almost nine thousand inhabitants live
degraded environment.

ff from society in dangerous homes and in a severely

Drawing by a child resident of Cañada Real

"Police Opression." The walls of Cañada Real represent a contain

ge, describing misery, violence, and social exclusion.

"Shop. Bread available."

IDA
DAN

“Woman means life.”

ViDA

VENTA
PRIVADA
OPEL
Special Days

The graffiti photographed in this visual chronicle appears on different walls throughout Cañada Real Galiana. The walls contain indications, pleadings, and aspirations, giving an account of the different frictions that exist in what is the largest and oldest informal settlement in the Autonomous Community of Madrid, which, according to EU data, is also the largest in Europe.

The linear settlement occupies 14 kilometers of an old 75-meter-wide cattle track of royal property road used for the transhumance of cattle property since the thirteenth century. Although this route is currently legally decommissioned, it is still public property and recognized as a cattle trail.

With the disinterested public administration, the territory was gradually "colonized" through the construction of houses, becoming a neighborhood to some 2,700 families.

The first inhabitants arrived just after the Spanish Civil War (1936–1939), at a time of big internal migrations. While the inhabitants of small villages too closely associated with the victor of the war were forced to flee to a larger city that would facilitate their anonymity, others relocated in search of work opportunities.

During the 1950s, Cañada welcomed around three hundred families, all settled in the northern part of the cattle route. They were working-class people with few resources but still nostalgic for what a rural area could offer: a small vegetable garden and some farm animals. They found it in Cañada.

And so the territory was slowly occupied by self-organized communities, all with a certain blind eye from the authorities who allowed them to settle down and build their precarious homes as the result of the state's own inability to offer affordable public housing.

The greatest growth occurred in the 1990s and the beginning of the 2000s, when the global economic crisis hit the country and, specifically, Madrid. Many people who lost their jobs and homes, as well as migrants and asylum seekers, had no other option but to move towards the urban margins and become part of an impoverished and degraded periphery.

This entire population has been historically neglected by the public administration, except in 2015–2019 during the mandate of Mayor Manuela Carmena, who developed a roadmap for achieving social inclusion through the fulfillment of the right to housing and the city, as well as enhancing the participation of all actors involved in the territory. Other than this brief moment of optimism, no realistic and consensual solutions have been offered. Segregation and exclusion have prevailed over the fulfillment of fundamental human rights.

At present, the situation is so socially vulnerable and environmentally abject that it is inconceivable that Cañada is part of the richest region in Spain.

The numbers are clear. According to UN-HABITAT, eighty percent of Cañada's almost nine thousand inhabitants live cut-off from society in dangerous homes (whether in the form of inadequate housing—self-built, substandard housing, or shacks) and in an environment severely degraded by illegal dumping, a lack of sewage systems, and quality public services.

Within this population is an even more vulnerable sector: the southern end of Cañada has been without electricity for more than two years (as of December 2022). The service had been provided by the regional government of Madrid but was denied for safety reasons. The families Cañada Real suspect that these supply cuts have more to do with the pressure exerted by neighboring developments that wish to evict the residents. Despite the complaints filed and resolved before the various national and international bodies, there has been no change. They are still in the dark and without electricity.

The walls presented in this collection of photographs represent a contained rage. They describe the misery, the explicit violence, the lack of resources, the social exclusion, the cultural diversity, the impossibility of registering the occupation of plots of land, even the serious linguistic deficiencies, and the fragile educational processes, but they also want to give space for hope.

The families of Cañada, together with different social organizations, political groups, and universities, have been weaving together possible and realistic strategies to improve and facilitate day-to-day life, demanding the fulfillment of fundamental human rights from political leaders, the ombudsman, and European organizations and committees.

And yet despite these efforts and international support, the situation remains unsustainable. With this small sample of "speaking walls," we hope to awaken a public conscience, change the way we look at things, and move towards a key question: what does this have to do with me?

Santiago Cirugeda is a social architect who questions the limits of legality and defining processes for social action to improve the city and tackle some of the problems facing residents. He is the founder of Recetas Urbanas, a design and advocacy collective of architects, lawyers, and social workers. Known for its self-build projects that rely on local participation for construction, the collective uses locally sourced second or third-hand materials to complete its mobile structures. Activating different areas of urban reality, its projects are at the same time highly functional and exploit the legalities surrounding the occupation of public space.

María Paz Núñez Martí is an architect and specialist in heritage recovery and rehabilitation and development cooperation. She coordinates the area of Habitat and Territory of the Research Group applied to development cooperation COOPUAH. She has been Technical Advisor to the Madrid City Council for the shanty town settlement of Cañada Real (2015–2019) and currently conducts applied research on spatial justice, urbanism, and citizenship from various civic platforms with political impact in the city of Madrid.

Architecture's Non-Nested and Elastic Scales

(15 min read)

Norilsk
69.3558° N, 88.1893° E

Iqaluit
63.7467° N, 68.5170° W

Inari
68.9062° N, 27.0278° E

Lola Sheppard and Mason White

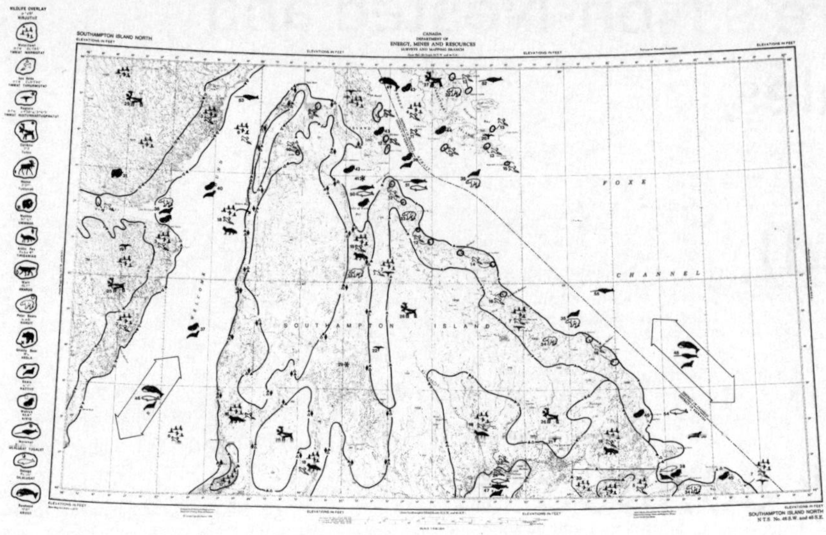

(FIG. 1A)
Wildlife Overlay, Southampton Island North, Department of Energy, Mines and Resources, Surveys and Mapping branch, 1974

The conventional language of architects, landscape architects, planners, geographers, and other spatial practitioners is the scaled drawing—the plan, the map, the section—coded or notated according to specific conventions, built upon the belief that scale is measured, objective, and represents the truth. Whether at the scale of the building, site, city, or territory, we assume that scales are nested into each other. But this assumption also implies a kind of shared geospatial reference point within a site and proposition. Equally, the framing of scaled drawings suggests that all that is needed to understand the image is bound within the frame and legible at the same scale. These presumptions render scaled representations of site as unbiased, able to shift without friction. However, this is both misleading and a missed opportunity to consider the entangled nature of various scales. How might architecture challenge the literalness of scale representation, and understand it as a narrative tool in which to embed the frictions of highly local and territorial spatial stories?

Unframed and Non-Nested Scales

The assumption of nested and fixed scales is particularly embodied in Charles and Ray Eameses' celebrated film *Powers of Ten and the Relative Size of Things in the Universe*, made in 1977 for the IBM corporation. The film begins with an overhead view one meter away from a couple having a picnic in a park. Every ten seconds, the camera zooms out, perpendicular to the ground, marking a distance that is ten times farther away. Each factor of ten is framed and nested inside the previous frame until the film reaches a distance of one hundred million light years. Then we are guided back to the beginning before zooming into the microscopic qualities of the main figure's hand, skin, and cells at 0.000001 angstroms. The camera's omniscient, unbiased eye remains focused on only what is visible and framed at each scale, ignorant of the more complex forces shaping the physical environment, especially any entanglements of geopolitics, economics, and cultural practices that might be happening between scales or

1 Laura Kurgan, "Representation and the Necessity of Interpretation," in *Close Up at a Distance, Mapping Technology & Politics* (New York: Zone Books, 2013), 19–36.

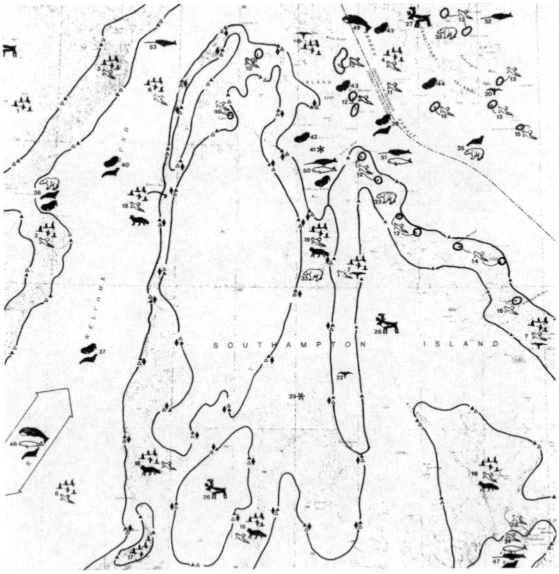

(FIG. 1B)
Wildlife Overlay, Southampton Island North, Department of Energy, Mines and Resources, Surveys and Mapping branch, 1974; from *Nunavut Atlas*, Canadian Circumpolar Institute and Tunngavik Federation of Nunavut, 1992, detail

at the periphery. Architect Laura Kurgan sees the film's scaling in and out by powers of ten as a precursor to the scaling ability of satellite imagery and military surveillance, or even our use of Google Earth. She argues that the film suggests objectivity when in fact "there is no absolute scale, just as there is no natural or logical starting or stopping point for the zoom ... every scale is relativized by its proximity to and distance from the next."[1] The couple on the picnic blanket are the literal "center" from which the camera seems to zoom out and in, and every scale is relativized by its proximity to and distance from the next. Charles Eames narrates each scale, describing what horizontal distance could be covered at what speed. The implication of the film is the promise of pure scalar relationships and hence absolute "truth," yet as Kurgan points out there is no basis for the process of zooming itself. She attributes the film as "an exercise in radical decentering," since the act of zooming in and out is itself a construct, literally and cinematically.[2] The framing of scales and any notion of a common reference point is at the root of the complex bias of nested scales. If, however, scale is understood as not absolute but infinite, we could embrace a notion of elastic scales and non-nested spatial relationships where the microscopic is understood in immediate relation to the bigger picture.

In contrast to the "objectivity" purported in the Eameses' film, French essayist Georges Perec invokes a much more subjective understanding of scales of inhabitation in his 1974 essay "Species of Spaces." He describes inhabitation in chapters: the bed, the bedroom, the apartment, the street, the neighborhood, the town, the countryside, the county, and so on.[3] At each scale, Perec reflects on the messiness of inhabitation, its entanglements, and how it fosters a sense of belonging (or not). Perec, like the Eameses, moves progressively outward in scale, albeit with less precision and more recognition of the nested and shifting scales of inhabitation experienced in daily life. These scales are neither framed nor measured, and Perec allows them, like life itself, to spill into each other. This idea contradicts the presumed exactitude promised by *Powers of Ten*. Instead, Perec proposes an understanding of scale that includes experience, memory, and engagement with the objects and spaces perceived.

Collapsing and Elastic Scales

The late Bruno Latour, in describing the network as a paradigm for understanding social and spatial relations, suggested the possibility of collapsing the near and the far, offering that "the first advantage of thinking in terms of networks is that we get rid of 'the tyranny of distance' or proximity."[4] Further, he suggests that "elements which are close when disconnected may be infinitely remote if their connections are analyzed," and vice versa.[5] In this understanding, local and global scales

2 Ibid., 20.
3 Georges Perec, "Species of Spaces," in *Species of Spaces and Other Stories* (London: Penguin Books, 1999), 5–96.
4 Bruno Latour, "On actor-network theory. A few clarifications plus more than a few complications," (English version), *Soziale Welt*, vol. 47 (1996): 4, www.cours.fse.ulaval.ca/edc-65804/latour-clarifications.pdf.
5 Ibid., 4.

can conflate, the near and far are relative and interchangeable, and the remote and immediate can be understood as relational and adjacent once their "connections are analyzed."

In architectural terms, Latour's tyranny of geography might be understood as the tyranny of linear scalar relationships, and the assumption that all things spatial can be measured, mapped, described, and framed objectively. Maps have been criticized as "the weapons of imperialism" because they are beholden to the viewpoint of the author whose role is to present the illusion of a singular objective perspective, which their seeming precision asserts.[6] In reality, maps are laden with omissions and biases; not least because they privilege the bio-physical rather than socio-cultural complexities which are much more challenging to visualize. Latour's notion of networks offers a counterpoint to the convention of the map and allows for the collapsing of scales to establish what might be called a truly shared, or common, proximity that embraces degrees of connectivity and refutes literal distances.

Anthropologist Anna Tsing similarly argues against the dogmatism of scalar precision, suggesting that it blocks our ability to understand heterogeneity and complexity. Conversely, non-scalability theory enables one to account for contingency and failure. Tsing claims that "it shows us the architecture of non-nesting, which is key to the (re)making of cultural diversity, capitalist and otherwise."[7] How do we document or represent the lived experience of poverty, or a particular spatio-cultural practice? How do we draw out (understand) and draw in (visualize) the material consequences of capitalism or the cultural consequences of colonialism? Here, conventional scalar drawings fail. Instead, scalar thinking requires an elasticity in terms of dimensions, but also with respect to the socio-cultural, economic, or political influences which are accounted for in drawings. Indigenous peoples, among other groups, have for decades challenged the tyranny of scalar documentation by counter-mapping practices through a non-western lens. Traditional knowledge and land use maps have been created with Indigenous hunting, gathering, fishing, and trapping groups as part of critical mapping practices and have served as tools for political activism to restore land rights. These counter-maps disprove the western imperial perspectives that deemed land "empty" save for its resource potential. Going beyond framed, scaled, static territory, Indigenous counter-maps reveal that the land is inhabited, practiced, active, and evolving. One of the most compelling examples is the

(FIG. 2)
Domestic model and territorial podium for Nuuk, Greenland, showing a series of distinct domestic rooms and territorial "rooms," photo Giorgio Lazzaro

6 J. B. Harley, "Maps, Knowledge, and Power," in *The Iconography of Landscape*, ed. D. Cosgrove and S. Daniels (Cambridge: Cambridge University Press, 1988), 277–312.
7 Anna Lowenhaupt Tsing, "On Nonscalability: The Living World Is Not Amenable to Precision-Nested Scales," *Common Knowledge* 18, no. 3 (Fall 2012): 505–524.

(FIG. 3)
Domestic spaces in Reyðarfjörður, Iceland, document a worker camp for aluminum smelting and the impacts of these activities on the territory, photo Giorgio Lazzaro

comprehensive *Nunavut Atlas*, published in 1992, (FIGS. 1A–1B) which describes Indigenous land use and critical wildlife areas that assisted Inuit in determining the specific portions of lands they would retain as part of the settlement of the Nunavut land claim.[8] Another example is the online interactive map Native Land, established in 2015 and directed by a majority-Indigenous board of directors, which describes Indigenous lands across the globe in terms of languages, treaties, and territories revealing the overlapping and entangled territories, histories, and cultures.[9] In a similar vein, geographer Claudio Aporta and Michael Bravo worked with Inuit elders to create Pan Inuit Trails, another online map developed in 2006 that documents trails, traditional place names, and historical events across Baffin Island.[10] The maps offer a contemporary record of Inuit mobility and occupancy of Arctic waters, coasts, and lands, including icescapes, and thus preserve knowledge while reasserting historical Inuit presence on the land.

Geographer Stuart Elden notes that: "Territory is itself a process, made and remade, shaped and shaping, active and reactive."[11] Much of this "process" is the ongoing negotiation for resources, the assertions of nation-states and claims made on behalf of Indigenous sovereignty. If counter-mapping has become an established practice which reveals the territory as process, is there an equivalent *counter-drawing* or representational practice at the scale of architecture, landscape, and urbanism? And how do such alternative representations enable us to draw out perceived proximities and connections, to challenge what we understand as near and far, local and global? Furthermore, can settler architects and urbanists participate in this process of counter-mapping? Whose stories are they telling, and from which perspective?

Elastic Scales

A recent project conducted in collaboration with Arctic Design Group, *Contested Circumpolar, Domestic Territories* (2020–2021), embraces a multi-scalar analysis of ideas of the domestic to understand patterns of living in the Circumpolar world at the territorial and the hyper-local simultaneously. It takes a material culture approach, which traditionally deals with the study of objects, resources, and spaces to understand how they reflect and define different societies. The relationship between people and things enables an understanding of production, consumption, and culture.

In the Arctic, where assertions of sovereignty, colonization, and geopolitical and

8 Rick Riewe, ed., *Nunavut Atlas* (Edmonton: Canadian Circumpolar Institute and the Tungavik Federation of Nunavut, 1992).
9 Native Land Digital, https://native-land.ca/.
10 Pan Inuit Trails map, co-directed by Claudio Aporta, Michael Bravo, and Fraser Taylor, advice www.paninuittrails.org/index.html?module=module.about.
11 Stuart Elden, *The Birth of Territory* (Chicago: University of Chicago Press, 2013).

(FIG. 4)
The Khrushchyovka apartment is the residential building block of Norilsk. The city exists for the sole purpose of nickel extraction; an extensive network of pipes, electrical grids, rail lines, and waste landscapes are the territorial evidence of this extraction

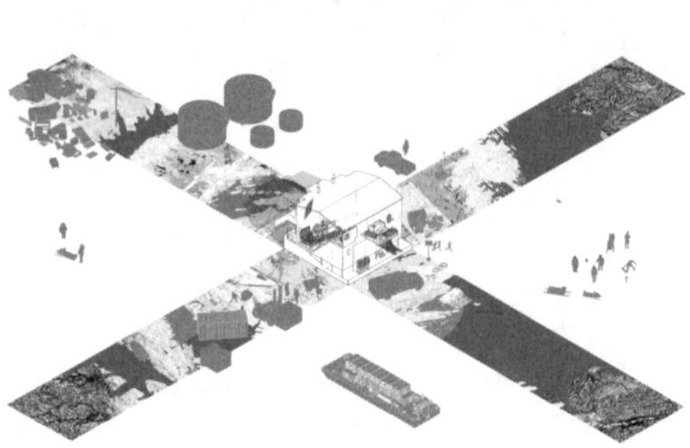

(FIG. 5)
The typical rental housing in Iqaluit and other Nunavut communities are the sites of extreme over-crowding of people and objects. Domestic life spills out, with snow-mobiles, boats, and other objects stored on site. Fuel, water tanks, and barges delivering the annual sea-lift remind one of the tenuous infrastructural links to the territory while residents traveling on the land remind one of the profound connection of domestic and the territory

capitalist forces have had particularly legible impact, the house is not necessarily home but rather imposed and often, in fact, the site of cultural trauma.[12] For Indigenous peoples, home not only extends beyond the confines of the house; the land is seen as "home," and family is "home" while the physical structure of the house often embodies a cultural erasure.[13] If we approach housing in the Arctic through a colonial lens—not dissimilar from how cultural theorist Dolores Hayden examined the home through a gendered lens or her contemporary Dianne Harris examined the home through a racial lens—the house becomes a forensic tool by which to understand local histories and serves as a magnifier of forces shaping the larger territory in which both house and home are situated. Furthermore, the history of housing in the Arctic is littered with ill-conceived, colonial, one-size-fits-all solutions largely developed by southern architects unfamiliar with the regions for which they designed. Most models of housing have been imposed by the state, whether to support resource extraction or to promote sovereignty through forced relocation or new settlements. In each instance, the architectural focus of the home is reduced to a basic shell protecting against climate but failing as a cultural and social interface situating domestic space within territorial space. Housing in the Arctic mirrors and crystalizes the complexities of the Circumpolar North. It is caught between notions of the local and the global, between Indigenous and colonial practices, between self-build and mass prefabrication. There appears to be no middle condition between these extremes. The objects which populate the domestic often represent the one realm in which residents retain agency over their environment. The expression of the domestic can be seen as a form of critical resistance; the manifestation of local cultures percolating up despite the orthodoxy and colonialism of so much of Arctic architecture.[14] *Contested Circumpolar* seeks to collapse the space between the room and the region. By linking domestic space to territorial space, a contemporary Arctic vernacular is revealed.

As authors of the project, we are not from the Circumpolar regions and hence relied on interviews with local residents and planners,

12 Frank Tester, "Inuit Homelessness: Knowing, Growing and going to make a difference," National Conference on Ending Homelessness, the Canadian Association to End Homelessness, November 11, 2018.

13 The work of Sami architect Joar Nango speaks to this powerful reclaiming of Indigenous domesticity. See among others Mimi Zeiger, "Interview: Joar Nango on Indigenous Architectures and Slippery Identities," *Pin-Up Magazine*, https://pinupmagazine.org/articles/interview-mimi-zeiger-joar-sami-architecture-joar-nango.

14 The work of Inuit artist Annie Pootogook drew intimate (and sometimes harsh) depictions of daily life. In one image, *Eating Seal at Home*, a family eats traditional country food on the floor, almost in defiance of how the colonially imposed northern houses were conceived.

(FIG. 6)
Domestic spaces in Sámi territory of Finland are often composed of ingenious repurposing of found elements, in this case an upturned boat hull becomes a workshop, photo Giorgio Lazzaro

travel and first-hand observations, documentary films, and photographs by others, as well as analytic drawings at various scales. The collected research synthesizes these spatial stories into three-dimensional models which document the spatial connections between the domestic and territorial scale. (FIGS. 2–3) Conceived like core-samples, eight stories of contested domestic and territorial inhabitation are told, one for each of the eight Circumpolar Nations. While in no way comprehensive, the three-dimensional models describe stories of inhabitation, movement, relocation, destruction due to climate change, housing inequality and over-crowding, but also celebrate local ingenuity, cultural and spatial practices of food, daily life, and community gathering, amongst others. The domestic-scaled models are conceived as X-rays into key spaces of houses. Specific objects highlight local adaptations which deal with the specificity of arctic climate, remoteness, environment, or which are expressions of local culture. The model podiums describe territorial infrastructures, landscapes, and geopolitical forces shaping each community.

The elastic scale between the domestic and the territorial is, for instance, visible in Norilsk, Russia, where the Khrushchyovka apartment block was deployed with almost ruthless efficiency across the city, its now aging concrete panels and foundations slowly cracking and failing. (FIG. 4) To combat the long dark winters, grim urban conditions, and evident ecological ravages, residents maintain artificial lights and greenhouses in their apartments synthetically reproducing natural environments indoors. Everywhere in the surrounding landscape, one is reminded that life in Norilsk exists for the sole purpose of nickel extraction. Both the Khrushchyovka apartments and the mines are supported by a complex network of pipes, rail lines, and electrical grids which traverse an ecologically ravaged landscape.

In Iqaluit and other Nunavut communities in Canada, on the other hand, a metaphorical X-ray into a typical housing unit reveals severe over-crowding: bedrooms strewn with mattresses, sustaining more residents than ever intended. (FIG. 5) Fuel and water tanks adjacent to the house are infrastructurally tethered to the fuel tanks and water reservoirs outside of town while snowmobiles remind one of the critical importance to Nunavummiut of going out onto the land.

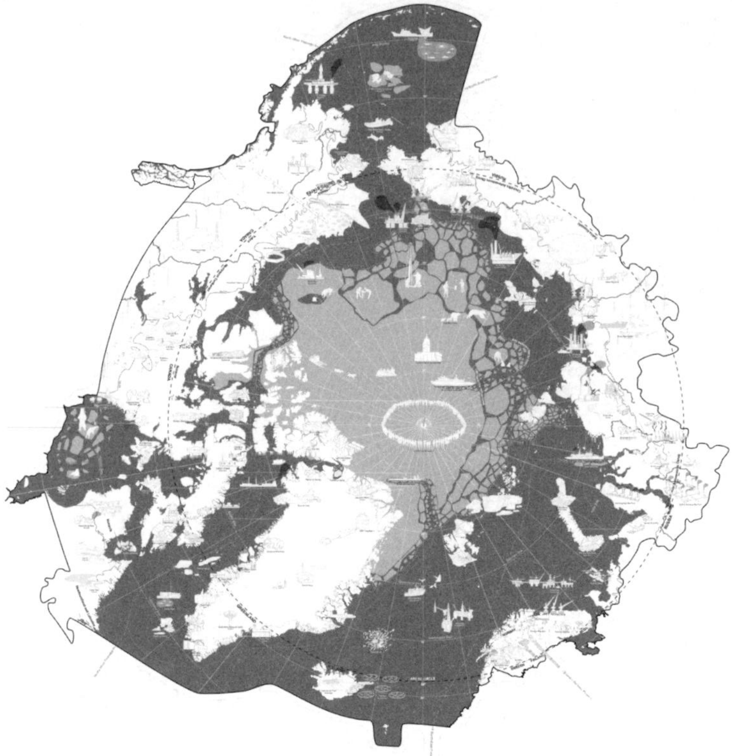

(FIG. 7)
Circumpolar map with integrated micro-narratives of contested territories

In Inari, Finland, the evidence of Indigenous ingenuity is legible in various domestic adaptations such as the repurposing of old boats for temporary shelter, the craftmanship of particular cooking tools from local wood, and the transformation of sleds. (FIG. 6) These adaptations are part of a long tradition of being on the land. Simultaneously, the local ecology is under threat from rail lines built to support ever-encroaching mineral extraction, a reminder of the friction of global capitalism on the hyper local.

In a context where so much of daily life happens either in the home or out on the land, *Contested Circumpolar, Domestic Territories* exposes the linkages of near and far, the local and the global, as sites of colonial contestation and Indigenous sovereignty, and seeks to reveal an *elastic middle scale.* (FIG. 7)

Non-Nested Scales

Urban theorists such as Neil Brenner have argued that we have entered an era of planetary urbanization, where "the urban can no longer be understood with reference to a particular 'type' of settlement space, whether defined as a city, a city-region, a metropolis, a metropolitan region, a megalopolis, an edge city, or otherwise."[15] One can no longer distinguish between densely populated urban regions and less densely settled zones of a region, nor between a territory, a continent, or the global. We see an argument that city, region, and territory are no longer embedded each in the other, but rather, work in elastic ways, such that the urban and the global are one. To embrace design in elastic and non-nested scales might offer an ability not only

15 Neil Brenner and Christian Schmid, "Planetary Urbanisation," in *Urban Constellations*, ed. Matthew Gandy (Berlin: Jovis, 2012), 10–13.

(FIG. 8)
An Ocean of WEEE: The geography of electronics material extraction, its subsequent product manufacturing, and ultimately its disposal reveal a fragmented globe; distinct leaders in extraction, manufacturing, consumption, and waste management corroborate economic and social disparity embedded in globalization

(FIG. 9)
Toxic Colonialism: The territories that form as part of the global archipelago of e-waste generate nodes of e-waste management, often in informal, un-regulated, and resulting in dangerous and toxic conditions. Key centers of disassembly are in Guiyu, China; Agbogbloshie near Accra, Ghana; and Shershah in Karachi, Pakistan, receive and recover the largest quantities of e-waste

to understand global and territorial networks, but also to envision productively disruptive local interventions.

Our global electronic production, consumption, and waste are one embodiment of these territorial processes and networks. As sociologist Jennifer Gabrys has written: "Just as there are material, social and economic infrastructure that support the growth and circulation of electronics, so too, are there elaborate infrastructures for removing electronic waste."[16] *States of Disassembly* (2017), followed the trail of impact of electronic waste at multiple scales. The premise of the research was to identify how these scales were co-planar rather than nested within each other. In addition, the research reveals the spatial politics of e-waste through extraction, corporations, and current waste logistics. This was undertaken at three non-nested scales using a counter-drawing technique. The impact of electronic waste globally offers three vantage points from which to observe the e-waste cycle: at the scale of the planet, the territory, and the product.

The largest scale reveals an archipelago of nations that are the primary consumers, distributers, and managers of e-waste. (FIG. 8) It identifies their co-dependence and distribution systems. The next scale reveals fragmented territories and regions that have become intertwined in the management processes of e-waste. (FIG. 9) This scale shows toxicity and labor practices. The smallest scale is of the product and its rare earths and metals. The drawing serves as a reminder that each electronic consumer object embodies a vast network of material resources emerging from toxic landscapes and nefarious labor practices. (FIG. 10) Each scale of e-waste reveals both the accumulation of objects and the formation of a distinct socio-political realm. Each of these collections represents a strata of our consumption habits. As discarded e-waste migrates in search of a place to rest,

16 Jennifer Gabrys, *Digital Rubbish: A Natural History of Electronics* (Ann Arbor: University of Michigan Press, 2011), vi.

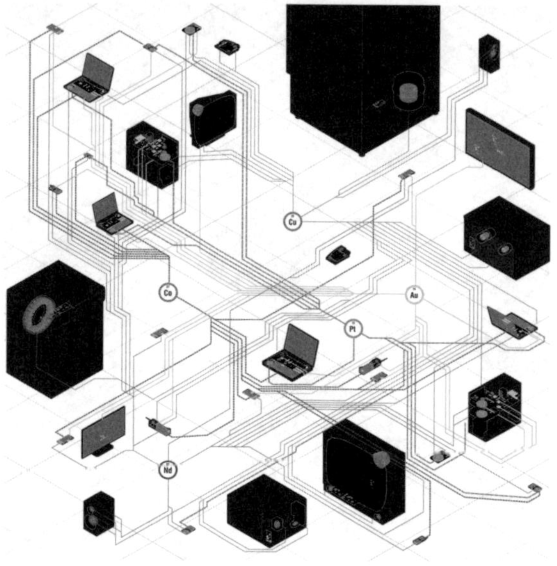

(FIG. 10)
From Product to Material: The products of e-waste are an array of devices and products fully entangled within our contemporary social and work culture. The preciousness and value of finite raw materials is great enough that recovery is not only necessary but also valuable.

it adheres to any carrier. Each scale exposes political and ecological complexities as well as an embedded toxic colonialism.

The geography of rare earth materials and other resources needed for electronics, its subsequent product manufacturing, and ultimately its disposal, reveals a fragmented globe. In the wake of increasing waves of e-waste, an archipelago of nations surfaces. Distinct leaders in extraction, manufacturing, consumption, and waste management corroborate economic and social disparity embedded in globalization. At each stage in the lifecycle of electronics, nations emerge as primary contributors. Despite the passage of the Basel Convention, few nations have the infrastructure in place to properly disassemble and dispose of their e-waste, in part because the cost of recycling is not yet offset by the value of the resources extracted. This results in the continued global shipment/transfer of waste from wealthier e-consumer nations to poorer e-waste receiver nations whose more informal economies, less regulated environmental controls, and inexpensive labor forces render the return on investment in disassembly viable.

The territories that form as part of the global archipelago of e-waste generate nodes of e-waste management, often in informal, un-regulated ways, and resulting in dangerous and toxic conditions. Key centers of disassembly include Guiyu, China; Agbogbloshie in Accra, Ghana (now closed); and Shershah in Karachi, Pakistan, receive and recover the largest quantities of e-waste. Within these informal centers, there are sites dedicated to burning, smelting, breaking, smashing, and other actions. The activities, necessary to disassemble and separate materials, generate chemical ecologies of toxic water, land, and air radiating outward from these sites. A precarious labor force of e-waste specialists is instrumental to the disassembly and chemical processes, yielding a contemporary form of toxic colonialism. These management sites produce three primary outcomes for materials: toxic waste, scrap recovery, or landfill.

Our territories are, broadly speaking, made up of three general uses: sites of production, consumption, and waste. Within each of the above-mentioned categories, there is a process of translocation, as materials in various states move from region to region, first assembled and, at the end-of-life, disassembled. The city, for example, is the preeminent site of consumption while production and waste sites are often peripheral and located out-of-view. This distinct partitioning of land use—separating consumption (clean) from production and waste (dirty)—is a consequence of contemporary capitalist landscapes and a privileging of consumption spaces as the space of public realm. The cycle begins with the harvesting of a material to manufacture products; the product is then consumed within conducive sites; and, once

17 Ibid., 4.
18 A version of this work was published in the 2017 Seoul Biennale Catalogue: Lola Sheppard and Mason White, "States of Disassembly: Electronics, Toxicity, and Territory," in *Imminent Commons: The Expanded City*, ed. Alejandro Zaero-Polo and Jeffrey Anderson (Barcelona: Actar, 2017), 406–414.

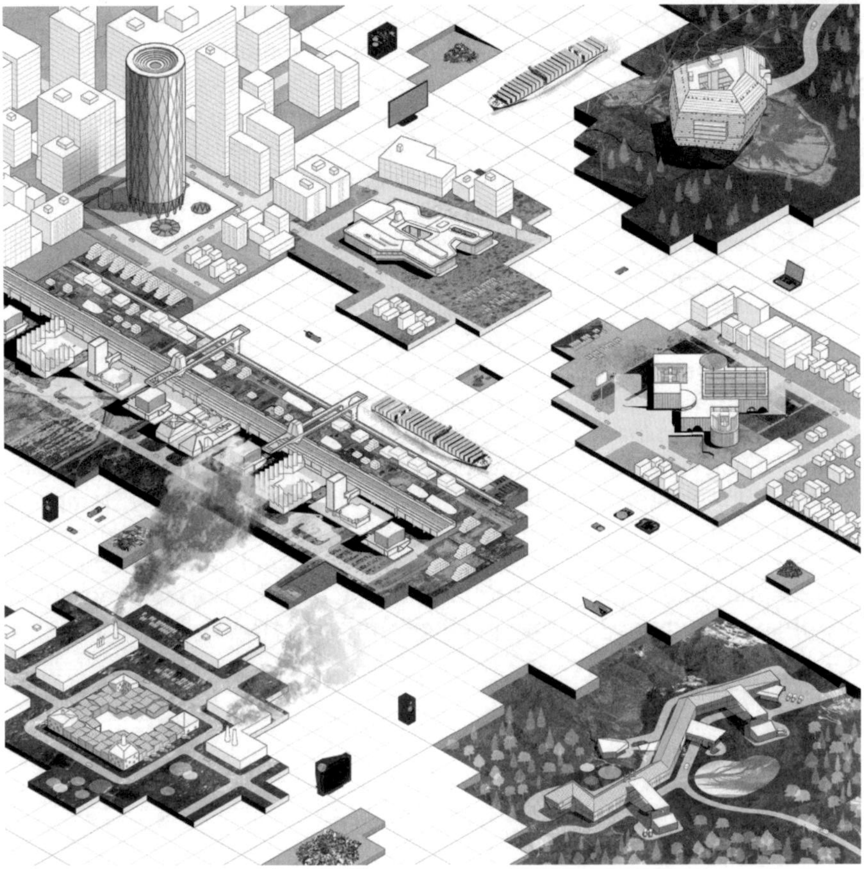

(FIG. 11)
Seven new typologies test new programmatic pairings and new forms of commons that might be fostered if we designed for the e-waste stream.

the product has expired, we seek a place to dispose of it. Locating this cycle reveals three general spaces: the mine, the city, and the dump.

As Gabrys notes: "The sedimentary layers of waste consist not only of circuit boards and copper wires, material flows and global economies, but also of technological imaginings, progress narratives, and material temporalities."[17] *States of Disassembly* exposes these entangled scales of analysis and spheres in order to propose a counter-narrative: a series of building and landscape types that recognize a possible e-waste commons—leveraging trends in reuse, repair, education, and entertainment. (FIG. 11) The drawings collapse scales, moving from the global to the local to the object, enabling us to test new programmatic pairings and new programmatic typologies and new forms of commons that might be fostered if we designed for the e-waste stream.[18]

With the rise of hacker culture and the increasing fascination in personal robotics, electronics is an integral part of modern entertainment culture. The Theatre of Disassembly brings together an assemblage of theatres under one roof for varying aspects of post-consumer electronics entertainment consumption. The theatres are composed as a series of stages and venues intended to host hacking battles, disassembly events, and demonstration classes. Theatres are raised off the ground, each one formally configured for specific activities. While the public circulates above, the ground remains an active space dedicated to electronic waste and its stewards who disassemble, construct, and repurpose it. A series of catwalks invite visitors to wander from one performance space to the next.

The current global e-waste stream is dependent upon the constant movement and shipping of waste. The Exchange Campus, capitalizes on this inevitability by offering a knowledge-based environment (campus) at the very port where materials pass through. It is divided by a central infrastructural material storage spine. The campus side contains courtyards, classrooms, disassembly stations, while the port side hosts container yards. All of these structures are connected in some way to the material archives spine, which offers compartmentalized storage of e-waste in various states of purity, from rare earths to copper to cobalt. The Exchange Campus becomes a space of waste interception and knowledge acquisition before post-consumer products clog up geographies downstream.

As our exurban contexts are frequently dotted with "big boxes" promoting electronics consumption, the WEEE-Market cloaks itself within that familiar context. It is conceived of as a public marketplace for e-waste materials, shifting retail from consumption of new products to the repurposing of post-consumer components and materials. Distributed within the large light-frame space are distinct volumes where workshops and tutorials in disassembly, repair, and reuse are offered. A cable-tray delivery system in the ceiling structure allows the convenient movement of components across the space and between nodes. WEEE-Markets leverage the growing hacker and recycling culture for a wider consumer base.

Rather than addressing the challenges of electronic waste streams through engineered solutions, *States of Disassembly* posits new public spheres—new architectures that offer a celebration of the act of disassembly. While not tied to a specific geography, the projects engage the nations of the Global North who have long displaced the impacts of their industrial consumption onto other nations. Situated in city centers, on the peri-urban edge, and in urban hinterlands, the projects are underpinned by a desire to make our collective footprint on the globe more legible and tangible, such that they might incite new actions locally. *States of Disassembly* considers how new typologies could activate localized commons, activate new publics, while fitting into global networks.

To embrace elastic and non-nested scales is to revel in, and reveal, the political, social, and economic frictions which exist as domestic and urban intertwine with the territorial and global. The projects presented here attempt to negotiate these scalar paradigms, attempting to think ambitiously at the scale of the territorial or the global while intervening within the specificity and constraint of the local.

Lola Sheppard and Mason White are architects and educators whose design research explores the role of architecture in rural and remote regions. Their work embraces the multi-scalar and non-scalar design thinking required to operate in these culturally and geopolitically complex regions while seeking the potential for emerging typologies that negotiate the frictions and intricacies of the local and global. Much of their research and design work is done in collaboration with Inuit and First Nations communities. They are co-founders of Lateral Office, based in Toronto. Lola teaches at the University of Waterloo and Mason teaches at the University of Toronto.

Visions for Architectural Demodernization

(15 min read)

Asmara and Aba Shawl
15.3229° N, 38.9251° E

Sicily
37.2303° N, 15.0227° E

Emilio Distretti and Alessandro Petti
Photographs by Luca Capuano

In the short docufilm *The Form of the City* (1974) Pier Paolo Pasolini is seen walking the sandy coastline of the Agro Pontino (Pontine Marshes) near Rome. He offers a critical reflection on the state of postwar society in the age of consumerism, mass media, and television. Against what he sees as the specter of looming decadence, Pasolini praises the lifeworld of Sabaudia, a rural town that only a few decades earlier had been sanctified by Mussolini as the symbol of *bonifica integrale* (integral reclamation) and the so-called "internal colonization" of Italy's southern lands.

As if a guide escorting a tourist, Pasolini confesses his genuine fascination with the rationalist and metaphysic forms of Sabaudia. It is, he tells us, a place in which, "you can feel that this city was built to live in; you can find ordinary families inside it, human beings, living creatures who are complete, entire and fulfilled in their humble circumstances."[1] Sabaudia had to be admired, Pasolini claims, because it was built "on a human scale" where—despite the form and history of its architecture—"there was nothing fascist in it." In other words, these colonial settlements have no roots in the regime that produced them, at least in the mind of Pasolini. They are instead "the expression of those same realities that fascism had tyrannically dominated, namely Italy's provincial, rustic, and preindustrial worlds."[2]

Pasolini was not alone in his fascination with the "beauty" of these cities; many other cinematographers, artists, and intellectuals have influenced the ways in which western societies have sought to rationalize the forms of modernist buildings designed and built under fascism, to the point of celebrating them as innocent urban stages for perpetuating self-indulgent, rose-colored narratives about violent pasts. These are cities whose forms are "disconnected" from the social and political

1 Laurent Matthey and Nicola Cantoreggi, "'The Form of a City': Pasolini and the Poetic Ecology of the Sign," *Space and Culture* 20, no. 4 (2017): 399–414.
2 *Pasolini and … the form of a city*, directed by Paolo Brunatto (1974).

context that produced them—a series of cinematic urban realities that could inspire a new meme of "fascist architecture without fascism," whereby the architecture that once served as the vehicle for fascism's segregationist and imperialist ethos is disembodied from its purpose. Such an attitude was instrumental during Italy's modernization and the racialized nature of the imperial project as it has played out in contexts not only including Libya and the Horn of Africa, but also the Italian peninsula, where the south of Italy was considered an internal frontier to be tamed and colonized.

Few places illustrate this condition better than the two areas that represent the beginning and end of Italy's imperial modernist project. The first example, Aba Shawl, the first Indigenous Eritrean urban settlement, was swallowed up when the Italians started to colonize the newly occupied territory and founded the city of Asmara (today's capital of Eritrea). As a result, Asmara became a site for European design projects, including many examples of fascist architecture (in the 1930s the city was known as Piccola Roma, or Little Rome). Aba Shawl, which before the Italian invasion was part of a cluster of four villages also known in Tigrinya as Arbate Asmare, was referred to by its colonizers as the city's "native quarter," where the Indigenous population was confined. The second example is located within Italy itself and takes the form of a series of rural settlements built by Mussolini's government to "modernize" Sicily's "backward" countryside. This so-called "internal colonization" was part of a capital-driven campaign for reclaiming arable land that mainly affected Italy's rural South. Through a synthesis of monumentalism, technological development, and industrial planning, the fascist regime planned designs for urban and non-urban reclamation in order to celebrate a fascist style of living. This program was launched in continuation of Italy's settler colonial ventures in Africa.

These sites—in Eritrea and Sicily's rural settlements—represent Italy's first colony (1889) and the last outpost of its fascist regime (1941). While symbolizing opposite architectural and spatial worlds, with Aba Shawl considered a "native quarter" and Sicily a "rural colony," both spaces reflect forms of modern violence. This essay is therefore a patchwork of tales, insights, and visions for spatial and epistemic twists that suggest a different vision for historical narratives, architectural preservation, and heritage creation. From Asmara to Sicily, we collected stories and testimonies and put forward alternative modes of representation and storytelling that vouch neither for the erasure of their fascist architectural traces and colonization nor for the celebration of their presumed absolute and universal aesthetic values but, rather, for the deactivation of their founding principles in order to narrate their histories in an anti-colonial and anti-fascist spirit.

Scene 1
In the "buffer zone" of Aba Shawl, Asmara

SCUOLA

Cinema Croce Rossa
TELEPHONE

CINEMA
IMPERO

We visited Aba Shawl in January 2019, having spent several days touring the city of Asmara.[3] Two years earlier, in 2017, UNESCO nominated Asmara a World Heritage Site, citing the city as "an exceptional example of early modernist urbanism from the beginning of the twentieth century and its adaptation to an African context." The area that UNESCO demarcated in its World Heritage list follows the perimeter of the original colonial master plan[4]—that is, the modernist-designed, segregated "whites-only" area of the colonized city. The Indigenous settlement of Aba Shawl is instead relegated to an outer "buffer zone."[5] Sticking to controversial principles in preservation of "authenticity" and "originality," the nominated preservation area includes the ancient villages pre-dating the colonial city while excluding the expansion and informal sprawl of Aba Shawl that followed the Italian occupation.

In the language of architectural and cultural conservation, a buffer zone refers to a belt of protection, a landscape that surrounds the nominated space and facilitates (bureaucratically, technically, and strategically) its preservation. The term is also suggestive of warfare and the separate areas between combatants. It is a concept solidly anchored in the tradition of western architectural knowledge, dating back to the Roman architect Vitruvius, who related the "demarcation of an abaton as an inaccessible space by the people of Rhodes around the statue of Artemesia"[6] —in a word, delineating the sacred from the profane. According to the 2008 International Centre for the Study of the Preservation and Restoration of Cultural Property (ICCROM) protocol, a buffer zone is a tool that disconnects the object of protection from external dangers. Aba Shawl's role and function is thus to serve as a no man's land to preserve the colonial city. The urban settlement of Aba Shawl is what remains of the quarter of the Piano Cafiero,[7] the cadastral master plan drawn and implemented by the Italian government in 1936,[8] which aimed to extend the demolition of Asmara's already segregated Indigenous quarters to give more "breathing space" to the city center where all the government buildings and National Fascist Party headquarters were located. The native population was thus relocated beyond the northern hills.

If the colonial city was built using a scale design and comprised open space, cinemas, factories, shops, bars, hotels, residences, and government headquarters all standing proudly as symbols of white dominance and fascist power, Aba Shawl featured none of these elements. The only thinking that went into the transformation of the area was that it had to be separated from the center of Asmara. In the eyes of the colonizers, Aba Shawl was viewed as everything Asmara was not: a "backwards" and "underdeveloped" "native quarter" full of danger.

Today Aba Shawl is a densely populated neighborhood, a maze of low, clustered homes, unpaved alleys, and narrow sandy and pebbled passageways that stand in contrast with the geometric and ventilated layout of the

3 The trip to Asmara saw the participation of artists, architects, researchers, and students of the Decolonizing Architecture Advanced Studies program at the Royal Institute of Art in Stockholm.

4 Edward Denison, Medhanie Teklemariam, and Dawit Abraha, "Asmara: Africa's Modernist City (UNESCO World Heritage Nomination)," *The Journal of Architecture* 22, no. 1 (2017): 11–53.

5 Asmara Heritage Project, "Asmara Proposed World Heritage Site: Integrated Management Plan 2016–2021" (Asmara–Eritrea 2016).

6 Michael Turner, "Introduction," in *World Heritage and Buffer Zones Patrimoine mondial et zones tampons, International Expert Meeting on World Heritage and Buffer Zones*, ed. Oliver Martin and Giovanna Piatti (Paris: UNESCO World Heritage Centre, 2008), 17.

7 Salvatore Cafiero was the chief architect sent by the regime to Asmara to complete the master plan originally drawn up by the then Italian city-chief engineer and head of public works, Odoardo Cavagnari. Between 1913 and 1916 Cavagnari "modernized the city" and set the basis for racial segregation. This segregation was implemented following the principles of modernist zoning inspired both by the Western Garden City movement–a method of urban planning in which self-contained communities are surrounded by greenbelts–and European models of class division, but this time manifestly based on race. The city was divided and segregated into three parts. The south and west of the city was designated for residential housing exclusively for Italians. The center of town was open to other Europeans and to Indigenous traders. This included a market hall and a mosque that were placed at the boundaries with a third district into which the Indigenous population was confined and segregated.

8 Sean Anderson (2017); Giuliano Gresleri, "Un progetto perduto e una capitale ritrovata. Asmara da Cesare Spighi a Vittorio Cafiero," in *Asmara: Architettura e pianificazione urbana nei fondi dell'IsIAO*, ed. Giulia Barrera, Alessandro Triulzi, and Gabriel Tzeggai (Rome: Istituto Italiano per l'Africa e l'Oriente, 2008): 42–48; Anna Nuzzaci, "Architecture and Town Planning in Italian East Africa During the Years of the Empire (1936–1941)," in *Urban Planning in Sub-Saharan Africa. Colonial and Postcolonial Planning Cultures*, ed. Carlos Nunes Silva (New York: Routledge, 2015): 129–44; Ferruccio Canali, "Asmara, lo sviluppo urbano della Milano 'Bianca' degli altipiani, dopo il nuovo piano regolatore di Vittorio Cafiero (e Attilio Teruzzi con la consulenza Alberto Calza Bini) (1937–1939)," in *Per Amor di Classicismo*, ed. Ferruccio Canali (Florence: Bollettino della Società di Studi Fiorentini, 2015–2016): 281–327.

modernist city. Although Aba Shawl is considered by many Eritreans to be the pulse of Asmara's identity, it still bears the stigma of an underserviced and unsafe ghetto. Many residents of Asmara do not want to live in or spend time there, and Eritreans are well aware that the ongoing divisions and social stigmas through which Aba Shawl is framed are issues that their communities still have to tackle: it is the need to fight "the colony within," whereby segregations and demonizations of the past still influence those of the present.

Since the UNESCO nomination, any restoration work must follow strict protocols to preserve the "original" architecture of Asmara, even down to the colors used to paint the exteriors of the city's buildings—in a bitter twist, color lines continue to be the organizing principle of life in Asmara. Today, walking into Aba Shawl and crossing the color line drawn by the Italian occupiers, one can feel how the nomination controversially reflects UNESCO's universalistic and Eurocentric values.

However, the exclusion by UNESCO did not provoke strong outrage, because—surprisingly—by placing Aba Shawl in the buffer zone, the Asmara nomination creates a new paradox. Instead of enforcing a protracted sense of exclusion and segregation, the inhabitants of Aba Shawl have developed an upside-down narrative whereby the current former colonial city, in order to exist as a heritage site, needs the shield of the Indigenous city. This challenges the conservationist logic that traditionally relegates a buffer zone to just another sanitary barrier. Walking through the alleys of Aba Shawl, you forget about the art deco and the theatricality of the former colonial city, and instead encounter life at a genuine human scale. Aba Shawl was born and has evolved organically without any master plan. Every religion and regional ethnic group constitute its urban fabric. This cultural openness grew in reaction to—and in spite of—the harsh conditions of racial segregation. The exclusion prompted by colonialism ignited a sense of solidarity among the residents of Aba Shawl: conviviality, as well as shared public and private spaces and properties (internal courts, rooms and dwellings), resources, and spirituality developed into respect and a sense of ownership.[9] Interestingly, the technocratic label of buffer zone can open a door for the inhabitants of Aba Shawl to reject the inherited dichotomies of their colonized past: white versus black, inside versus outside, public versus private.

Many of the congested and clustered dwellings are built around internal communal courtyards shared by different families, where people gather and guests are welcomed. This system of internal courts produces a series of communal spaces shaped and inhabited by extended families and bound together by neighborliness. On the one hand, the houses have relatively small rooms and are typically cluttered and crowded. On the other hand, the internal courtyards created by these houses echo the traits of Islamic architecture, offering important "breathing space" and multiple functions, a balance between respect for traditional architecture and its use. Aba Shawl's culture of communal living is well represented by this system of internal courtyards, which offers a material configuration of the ways in which residents interpret, experience, and practice care, reciprocity, and hospitality.

Many residents, after welcoming us into their courtyard, engage with our questions: how do they feel about preserving the colonial city and the symbols of their oppression? "Well, we built it and we own it," they reply sardonically. There is a big truth to this response: generations of Aba Shawl's residents hold memories of the city's realization. Construction was carried out by laborers from Aba Shawl who dug trenches for water and sewage pipes, installed telegraph cables, laid railway track, and paved streets. Many Aba Shawl women provided Italian families with domestic labor, working as maids and carrying

9 For a more comprehensive history of the quarter, see "A short note on Aba Shawl" by Alemseghed Tesfay.
10 Denison et al, "Asmara: Africa's Modernist City."

out daily housework. [10] Retrieving memories and reappropriating the narrative of exploited Eritrean labor is an act of reclaiming heritage. The reiteration of a collective narrative of the production of the city, rooted in the experiences of unfree labor, allows the residents of Aba Shawl to imagine an epistemic twist of the divisions and compartmentalization projected by fascist Italy's colonialist optics and the modern architecture built to stand as its symbol. In this narrative recasting they are not segregated from the city, but integral to its creation. Without them, there might have never been a city for UNESCO to hope to preserve. By proclaiming themselves as the guardians of this heritage, they break the exclusion previously imposed on them.

Scene 2
Rural colonies in Sicily

BORGO
ANTONIO BONSIGNORE

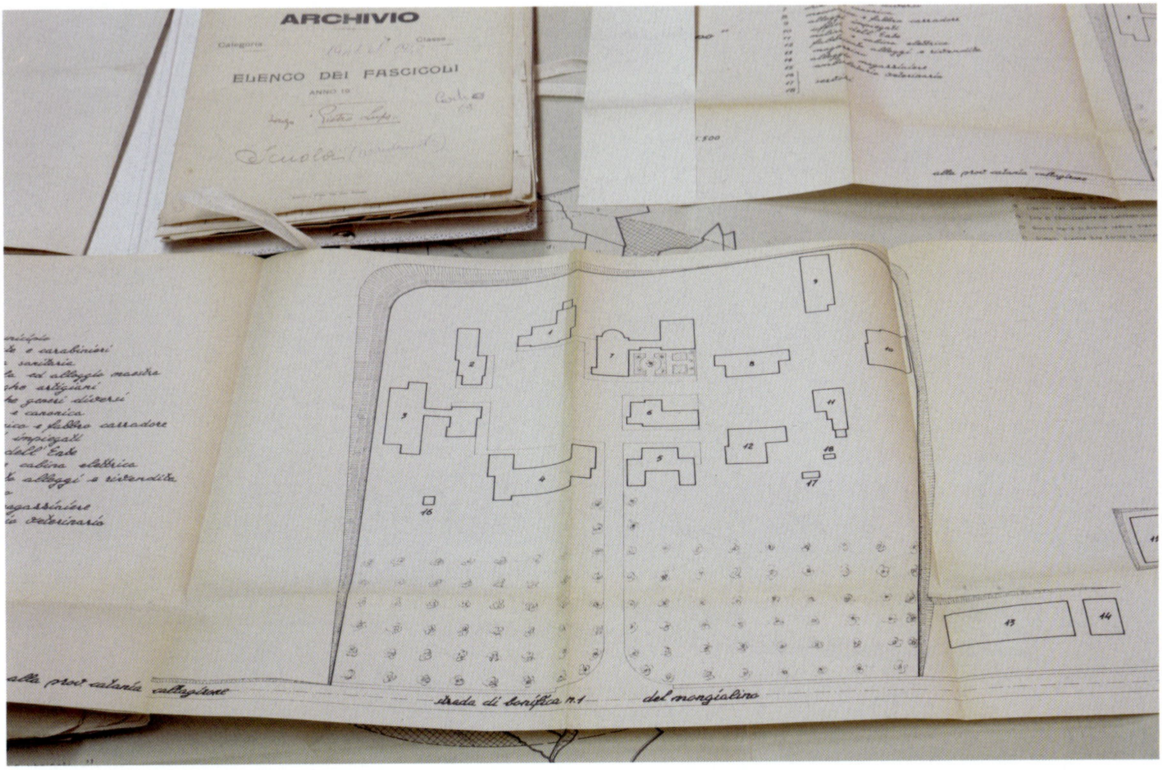
ARCHIVIO
Categoria
Classe
ELENCO DEI FASCICOLI
ANNO
strada di bonifica n.1
del mongialino

In June 2021, with Aba Shawl still vivid in our minds, we visited the internal rural lands of Sicily, first stop Borgo Gallea, a rural settlement in the province of Agrigento. There is no one else around: as we walk towards the only open cafe, the square and the buildings appear empty and the facades show traces of fresh plaster and recent renovation. When we order espressos at the counter, the young barman cannot help but ask: "You know who built all this, don't you?"

In 1940, the Italian fascist regime founded its last agency in Sicily, the Ente di Colonizzazione del Latifondo Siciliano (ECLS).[11] Between 1940 and 1943, ECLS built more than 2,000 homesteads and completed eight new towns in Sicily. They were built as replicas of the same structures and planimetries that had already appeared on African soil. All had the buildings of the Ente, piazzas, schools, fascist party headquarters, churches, pharmacies, artisan workshops, and restaurants.[12] To celebrate the fictitious unity between the colonies in Africa and the south of Italy, many of the Sicilian villages took the names of fascist martyrs, soldiers, and settlers who died in Ethiopia during the colonial war of occupation.

While on the one hand, the construction of settlements in the Sicilian countryside were supposed to tackle the needs of agrarian change, the fascist reform of the *latifondo* did not lead to the redistribution of land to peasants and farmers. On top of that, the internal colonization of the South, as well as Italy's settler colonial projects in Africa, were short-lived: the end of the Second World War also brought the formal end of fascism. Italy "lost"[13] its colonies while the many Ente scattered across the south of the peninsula were progressively shut down or reformed.[14] The word "colonization" was then "secularized" and replaced by "development." The *new* Ente was re-invented to again tackle the unsolved problem of land restitution, and despite the echoes of fascist rhetoric, it was celebrated by Italy's newly formed democratic institutions. However, southern *latifondista* were not defeated and managed to get parts of the expropriated land "re-assigned." Thanks to local mobsters who took back control of large portions of the area, most infrastructural projects, such as irrigation, drainage, aqueducts, roads, and railroads were kept under the same coercive control of wealthy landowners. In this scenario, most of Sicily's rural settlements were abandoned to a slow decay, and the surrounding areas were depopulated by new waves of outward migration.

After decades of neglect, the rural towns designed by the regime attracted the attention of local, regional, and central governments. Since 2007, a project entitled "La via dei Borghi" has sought public funding to restore these fascist settlements. The program has been promoted particularly by right-wing (but not only) regional governments as a nostalgic celebration of fascist ideals and the "uncontested beauty" of modernist architecture—all done to boost Sicily's rural tourism. Over the past decade some municipalities have secured funding for an architectural restoration of "clean" and "authentic" buildings, following a traditional preservationist approach that looks at modern architecture as an isolated object, an aestheticized icon to be admired for its formalist features.

The renovation of Borgo Bonsignore has become the flagship of that project. The town

11 The entity was created to reform the *latifondo*, for centuries the predominant agricultural system of production in southern Italy. These consisted of large estates of arable land owned by local noble landlords. Living far from their possessions, these landowners used local middlemen and hired thugs to sublet their land to local peasants and farmers who needed land for self-sustenance. Fascism sought to transform this very unproductive, outdated (and exploitative) system, forcing a wave of modernization. The fascist Minister of Agriculture Giuseppe Tassinari made clear that the colonization was both a state and private initiative: the state would invest important sums to build and maintain roads, aqueducts, wells, and farmhouses, while settler families would gain full ownership over the new-built private properties. See Giuseppe Tassinari, "La colonizzazione del latifondo siciliano," Conferenza tenuta in Palazzo Vecchio, 7 January 1940.

12 See Emilio Distretti and Alessandro Petti, "The Afterlife of Fascist Colonial Architecture: A Critical Manifesto," *Future Anterior* 16, no. 2 (Winter 2019): 46–58.

13 Due to a series of military defeats during the Second World War, Italy was forced out of Libya and the Horn of Africa by the Allies supported by Indigenous movements of liberation.

14 While the Ente in Libya was formally abolished only in 1961 (ten years after Libya's independence) the ECLS was reformed in 1950 and renamed the Ente per la Riforma Agraria in Sicilia. This led to the creation of a new institution, the Ente di Sviluppo Agricolo (ESA) in 1965.

was originally built in 1940 and named after a *carabinieri* officer who died in the Battle of Gunu Gadu in 1936 during the imperial war that Italy fought against Ethiopia. As we walk around the empty square, the whole settlement is literally wrapped in scaffolding. Despite the many tarpaulins covering its facades and arches, it is impossible to ignore the recently installed plaque commemorating the settler-martyr, as well as the heavy coat of stucco on the facade of the former *casa del fascio*. Here, restoration work is anchored to reviving the cinematic and metaphysical city, to the point that only a few years ago even global corporations such as Google rented the Borgo and transformed it into a stage for celebrities and business leaders.

But like in any theatrical performance, there is always an element of smoke and mirrors, and the stage of the Borgo is indeed designed for multiple illusions and deception. The undergoing restoration of the settlement's facades is again perpetuating an image of preservation where "alterations" are banned and forbidden. But what happens behind the curtain? Behind the attempts to protect the outward appearances of fascist architecture?

Over the years, with the failures of the agrarian reform and the closure of the new Ente of Development, the school and other buildings in the Borgo have gradually been reappropriated by local families. And behind the facades, informal changes to the interior design have organically followed: while outside, the original plaster of the buildings has slowly crumbled, on the inside, kitchens have been moved, walls knocked down, and new bedrooms added. Against a destiny of decay, these so-called illegal residents have maintained the buildings and the settlement, preserving without preservationists.

Conflicts among squatters and local municipalities always arise as questions of preservation resurface. Similarly, in the settlement of Borgo Cascino, near Enna in the center of Sicily, we hear of fraught relations between the few remaining residents and public officials around issues of care and maintenance. An old couple who has squatted in the Borgo for more than fifty years faced eviction when the local government planned restoration works. By keeping the settlement livable they eventually negotiated their indefinite right to stay. The result is another blow to an already weakened rhetoric around a type of conservation that cares for facades but ignores the lives that exist behind them and refuses to recognize the marginal communities performing *unruly* preservation—unofficially and with no public status, with no predetermined expertise or set of specific skills.

What is most striking about the fascist rural settlements of the Sicilian countryside is that despite their differences (some are abandoned and in ruins, some are homes to squatters or only half-populated) there is a common denominator: in those places the modern distinction between public and private spheres repeatedly blurs—or better, it collapses. While this could be explained as an outcome of the widespread lack of trust among the local population in its public institutions and governing bodies, the erosion between private and public life in the Borghi can—like at Aba Shawl—offer the opportunity to reverse conventional ideas about preservation, heritage-making, and design.

In the summer of 2021 we inaugurated a summer school in the former fascist settlement of Borgo Rizza. Working with the courageous municipality and residents of the nearby town of Carlentini, the school aims to produce, discuss, and imagine practices and strategies of (non)preservation, reappropriation, *profanation*, and decolonization of what we call a "difficult heritage."[15] We start with simple questions in order to re-frame the historical narrative around colonial and fascist architectural heritage: is it possible to subvert the original function of these settlements? How to

15 See Emilio Distretti and Alessandro Petti "Architectural Demodernization as Critical Pedagogy: Pathways for Undoing Colonial Fascist Architectural Legacies in Sicily," in *Architectural Dissonance*, edited by L'Internationale online and daas: https://www.internationaleonline.org/research/decolonising_practices/208_architectural_demodernization_as_critical_pedagogy_pathways_for_undoing_colonial_fascist_architectural_legacies_in_sicily/ internationale.

transform these sites into antidotes to fascism? Can we imagine heritage-making as a relational praxis that manifests beyond and despite experts in preservation/conservation?

Working and operating at the threshold between public and private spheres, participants of the school (residents, local and international students, artists, curators, immigrants, and refugees) collaborate to create communal, safe, and intimate spaces of learning and exchange that challenge the monumentality and rigid formalism of the surrounding fascist architecture. In an inaugural meeting participants set the pace of a coproduction of multiple spaces of learning. A series of *hassira* carpets (from the Al Khalil market in the West Bank Palestine) were laid down on the square to mark the space of our conversations. (In Palestine, and in the Arab Muslim world in general, a *hassira* is a decorated carpet that can be used for prayer or to establish comfortable outdoor seating areas, especially under the shade of olive trees when it is time for harvest.) Around the rugs a series of second-hand armchairs, sofas, and dining chairs donated by Carlentini residents were placed to form outdoor living rooms where people could gather, meet, and share.

The school seeks to return the Borgo to a common use—where the spheres of privacy, vulnerability, intimacy, and domesticity blur into the public realm as collective rituals. The former post office has been converted into a dormitory, and a mobile external kitchen[16] provides space for cooking sessions and opportunities for shared domesticity. Sleeping, cooking, and communal living become ordinary practices that somehow contribute to the gradual erosion of the divisions embodied by fascist architecture that relegated domesticity away from the public and banned intimacies and vulnerability from public life.

Through this we want to recognize and understand how the discursive (cultural and social) legacies of fascism survived architectural monumentality, and went further beyond it. Against a dehumanizing architecture, and cultures of masculinity and patriarchy that survived the end of fascist monumentalism, the school celebrates the town as a new space for the continuing heritage constituted by its participants. That heritage is now playing out in the application to rename the municipality Borgo EX. Through this collaborative process, we can ensure that the memory of an irredeemable and violent past is never forgotten while honoring the Borgo's present reality, in which it is already being used for something else and in continual transformation.

Epilogue: On Architectural Demodernization

The entangled histories of the irreverent gazes and counter-discourses on heritage-making and preservation from Asmara to Borgo EX show how fascist architecture must be understood as a branch of the European colonial/modern project of civilization, exploitation, and dispossession. Although there is widespread agreement around the fact that modern architecture (and its spatial reordering) was instrumental in the formation of colonialist domination, architectural modernism continues to be celebrated as a universal instrument of liberation for its progressive social agenda. While the terms modernity, modernization, and modernism are used interchangeably to celebrate and describe processes of social and infrastructural development, progress, democratization, and individual emancipations, whatever exists outside this perimeter is still stigmatized as anti-modern and traditional. Shaped around such universalizing norms and regulations, architectural modernism was meant to "save" society from political and social illness embodied by tradition.

We wish instead to embrace other ways of heritage-making that do not have modernism as a point of reference. Contrary to interpretations that want to reduce the world to binary oppositions (nature vs culture, public vs private, developed vs underdeveloped, the city vs the countryside), we suggest

16 The mobile kitchen is designed and built by Marginal Studio, Palermo, 2022.

"demodernization" as a practice that rejects the modernist dichotomy. "Demodernizing" does not relate to any anti-modernism. On the contrary, a "demodern option" acknowledges other ways of seeing and being conscious of the world, where modernity is simply not considered an unavoidable destiny, and modernist architecture a sacred space whose original use and design cannot be reversed. Instead, it calls for the profanation of those separations, disconnections, and isolations that are embodied and reflected by architectural modernism. By opposing an aggressive universalism, we have witnessed—and also practiced— demodernization as a method of epistemic desegregation. We see its application as both *discourse* and *praxis*, to invent forms of the reappropriation and reuse of modern (colonial and fascist) architecture.

Posing the question of demodernization means, first and foremost, understanding it in synchrony with the question of decolonization and recognizing that decolonization cannot exist without questioning the myriad other segregations that rippled (and still do) across geographical hemispheres. In so doing we suggest foregrounding "decolonization" in relation to "demodernization" beyond, and despite, colonially imposed geographical divides. Demodernization is also an epistemic reorganization of these divides, spaces, and architectures, and a call for the desegregation of colonial fascist heritage from its history. And it is, above all, a shift of consciousness, one that intends to undo the rationality of zoning and compartmentalization enforced by colonial modern architecture and urbanism. It addresses different ways in which people can potentially engage critically with their legacy and heritage, and heal a fracture between worlds deliberately set apart. It is about imagining how we can empower ourselves to reorient the narratives over the fascist colonial heritage, and reunite disconnected histories and experiences across the North/South divide.

Emilio Distretti is a researcher, writer, and educator. He is Research Tutor at the RCA School of Architecture, London, and a postdoctoral fellow in History and Theory of Architecture and Urbanism at the University of Basel. He engages with critical research methodologies and pedagogy centered around the entanglements between repair, reparations, and decolonization in the Mediterranean basin and in the Horn of Africa. In his writings and collaborations, he deploys and narrates the public dimension of architecture as a space and a tool for imaginative futures and repair from colonialism and its racialized, social, and economic aftermaths, a space for critical knowledge production around preservation. His work features in journals, books, and magazines including *Cabinet*, e-flux, *the Journal of Architecture*, *Future Anterior*, and *Antipode: A Journal of Radical Geography*. He collaborates with the art collective DAAR and with RIWAQ Centre for Architectural Conservation.

Alessandro Petti is Professor of Architecture and Social Justice at the Royal Institute of Art in Stockholm and co-director of DAAR (Decolonizing Architecture Art Residency), an architectural studio and residency program centered around the relation of politics and architecture. His recent books include *Refugee Heritage* (Art and Theory, Stockholm 2021) and *Permanent Temporariness* (Art and Theory, Stockholm 2019).

Luca Capuano is a photographer and educator. UNESCO, the Italian Ministry of Cultural Assets and Activities, and the Bangkok Embassy are just a handful of the well-known institutions he has worked with. His projects range from photo essays documenting Italian cultural heritage to shoots and ad campaigns for designer brands. His photos have been exhibited at the Seoul Biennale of Architecture and Urbanism, Abu Dhabi Nyuad Art Gallery, and Berlin Institut für Architektur, among others. He teaches photography at the Isia Institute of Urbino.

መዕረፍ ኣጋይሽ ብሪስቶል
BRISTOL
PENSION

Cinema Croce Rossa
TELEPHONE
TELEPHONE

EDITORS
Andrea Börner, Cristina Díaz Moreno, Efrén García Grinda, Baerbel Mueller, Institute of Architecture at the University of Applied Arts Vienna

fora-ontheurban.net
fora@uni-ak.ac.at

forA on the Urban is a project rendered possible by the University of Applied Arts Vienna, conceptualized and produced by the Institute of Architecture (I oA).

WITH CONTRIBUTIONS BY
Luca Capuano, Santiago Cirugeda, Emilio Distretti, Keller Easterling, Phineas Harper, Konstantin Kim, Alexia León, Hira Nabi, Ou Ning, María Paz Núñez Martí, Alessandro Petti, Nasrine Seraji, Lola Sheppard, Steloo, Xu Tiantian, Mason White

MANAGING EDITOR
Sarah Handelman

PUBLICATION MANAGEMENT
Roswitha Janowski-Fritsch

CONTENT AND PRODUCTION EDITOR
Katharina Holas, Birkhäuser Verlag, Vienna, Austria

PROOFREADING/COPYEDITING
Sarah Handelman

GRAPHIC DESIGN
Studio Lin

PRINTING
Holzhausen, the book-printing brand of Gerin Druck GmbH, Wolkersdorf, Austria

PAPER
Munken Polar 90 gsm, Magno Gloss 90 gsm, Munken Polar 170 gsm, SH Recycling 350 gsm

LIBRARY OF CONGRESS CONTROL NUMBER: 2023947260

Bibliographic information published by the German National Library. The German National Library lists this publication in the Deutsche Nationalbibliografie; detailed bibliographic data are available on the Internet at http://dnb.dnb.de.

ISBN 978-3-0356-2849-4
e-ISBN (PDF) 978-3-0356-2851-7

Im Westfeld 8, 4055 Basel, Switzerland
Part of Walter de Gruyter GmbH, Berlin/Boston

9 8 7 6 5 4 3 2 1 www.birkhauser.com